DESIGN
KNOWLEDGE
MANAGEMENT
SYSTEM

A PRACTICAL GUIDE FOR IMPLEMENTING ISO 30401 KMS STANDARD

DESIGN KNOWLEDGE MANAGEMENT SYSTEM

A PRACTICAL GUIDE FOR IMPLEMENTING ISO 30401 KMS STANDARD

AUTHORED BY
SANTHOSH SHEKAR

PENMAN BOOKS
A BOOK PUBLISHING COMPANY

PENMAN BOOKS

Office No. 303, Kumar House Building,
D Block, Central Market, Opp PVR Cinema,
Prashant Vihar, Delhi 110085, India
Website: www.penmanbooks.com
Email: publish@penmanbooks.com

First Published by Penman Books 2021
Copyright © Santhosh Shekar 2021
All Rights Reserved.

Title: Design Knowledge Management System
ISBN: 978-93-90156-81-8

I want to thank all the ancient seers, sages, ancestors, gurus for contributing knowledge about Self. I want to thank my teachers, guides, parents for leading me to the right path.

I want to thank all my previous and current Organizations, Colleagues and Managers for enriching my life with the opportunities to work and learn in their association.

I want to thank the ISO 30401 KMS Organizing Committee and Core working group for establishing the first version of the Knowledge Management Standard. I pay my respect and deepest gratitude to everyone who has contributed and expanded this KM field, and has influenced me in one way or the other.

I want to thank my Wife and Daughters for their boundless love and eternal support without which I would have not been motivated to write this book.

ॐ || Om Sarvhe Jana Sukhina Bavahntu || Let the whole human race prosper and be at peace!

Santhosh Shekar

CONTENTS

ABOUT THE AUTHOR

Santhosh Shekar has been a Knowledge Management practitioner for over 20+ years. During this professional journey of more than two decades, he has worked in various industries like Information Technology, Business/Knowledge Process Outsource, Finance, Insurance, Banking, Pharmaceuticals, Government, Media, Oil and Gas, etc. At present, he works in oil and gas company, Oman as KM Architect and also advises individuals and organizations on ISO Knowledge management Standards.

He is also the second person to be accredited with ISO 30401 Auditor Certification from Dr. Ronald (Ron) McKinley, PhD, MBA, SPHR (ICEE-International Center for Enterprise Engagement). Santhosh holds the authority to certify organizations and individuals on the basis of ISO 30401 Knowledge Management requirements. He has been certified as the Innovation Practitioner and Leadership Fellow from the UK-based Innovation and Knowledge

Exchange, Certified Knowledge Manager from Knowledge Management Institute, US.

Santhosh has been a key contributor to the field of knowledge management. He has been actively and passionately involved in developing Knowledge Management Systems for teams, designing Knowledge Management System architecture at the enterprise level, developing Lessons learned systems, developing Learning management frameworks for enterprises and rolling out KM for largescale to small projects. All such milestones have equipped him with fulfilling and enriching experience along with the addition of practical insights to his treasure trove of knowledge. This has helped him in achieving breakthroughs from the barriers of organizational structures, social structures, psychological barriers, technological barriers and knowledge visibility barriers.

He was born and brought up in the Silicon Capital of India, Bengaluru, and now works at the serene landscape of Oman. He is married and has two children. When he was 16, he developed a unique skin condition called vitiligo, which led him to the path of introspection of self and question the purpose of his life. His passion for Knowledge Management also fueled his inquisitiveness to learn more about psychology, sociology, organizational management, history, technology and many more fields to develop a holistic KM approach.

Academically, he is an Engineer and a Diploma holder in Electronics and Communication. His current mission is to make KM function an integral part of every organization globally.

For more details please visit: http://santhoshshekar.com

REVIEWS AND QUOTES

There are dozens of books and bodies of knowledge on how to design Knowledge Management Systems. However, this is the first book to speak in the language of the KM ISO standard 30401, and therefore has two unique advantages: easing the design of such systems for those who seek for ISO certification; and, serving as the North Star to excellence in KM, for whoever wishes to rely on the global collaborative knowledge of a first-class team of experts who designed the standard.

—Dr. Moria Levy, ISO 30401 Project Leader

~ ~ ~

Many organizations implement improvement initiatives through a set of projects that are not well connected and are not in response to the strategy. Shekar's insights highlight how to strategically connect with the improvement programs in a way that they inform strategy creation, using examples, practical templates and the ISO Knowledge Management Systems Standard as a guide. This is a powerful shift in mindset and an excellent place for the KM novice to start, whether they intend to achieve certification, or just apply the KM principles to enhance performance.

– Dr. Arthur Shelley, Founder, Intelligent Answers, Author-KNOWledge SUCCESSion

Unlike some Knowledge Management (KM) authors who focus on academic precision at the expense of clarity, Santhosh Shekar maintains a commendable focus on practical guidance and advice. Assembling a wealth of material from his decades of experience, Shekar provides extensive "how-to" detail that should abundantly satisfy even the most meticulous KM practitioner. Numerous process guides, checklists, and a detailed case study are presented to the reader and neatly aligned to ISO 30401 requirements, resulting in a comprehensive implementation guide that never feels overbearing or unwieldy.

—Stephen Bounds, Founder- RealKM Magazine

~ ~ ~

Santhosh brings a holistic perspective to the field of Knowledge Management. He brings extensive life experience in addition to his KM and organizational experience. Lucky are those who get a chance to work through the ISO 30401 certification with him.

Collison Eng Corney's book on ISO 30401 brought a lovely metaphorical way to embrace the KM standard. As a partnership across books, Shekar offers both a holistic and detailed view of knowledge management. Readers may appreciate both the strategic and tactical approaches that are shared.

KM is difficult. It is a difficult field to understand, practice, design, implement, mature, sustain and evaluate. In this book, Shekar brings clarity and purpose to this challenging field by personally sharing his experiences and deepest insights. What a pleasure to read, learn and practice KM together.

This is a must-read book for anyone looking to understand the field of Knowledge Management, and how to implement it with regard to ISO 30401. Shekar shares decades of KM experience through stories, strategic approaches and detailed implementation tactics. You'll find models, and lists of questions, for immediate learning and application. Let's keep the KM conversation and momentum going!

—**John Hovell, Managing Director & Co-Founder at STRATactical International LLC**

~ ~ ~

This book explores KM from the ground up – enabling beginners and practitioners to step through all the

considerations of a Knowledge Management System, including building in and on the ISO standard.

The guidance is a lot more than implementing and complying with the standard

Plenty of examples and checklists fill out example details to support the fundamentals of KM, KMS design and implementation in a variety of organizations.

—**Ian Fry, Chair Australian KM Standards, Director, KM Consultant Knovo- Australia, Fry Systems Owner**

~ ~ ~

It's a handy practical guide on how to go about implementing Knowledge Management, which in turn can help enhance the business's productivity & manpower efficiency through more effective knowledge & learnings transfer. A lot of the messages in this book resonate well with my experience of working with Santhosh on implementing knowledge transfer.

—**Ali Lamki, Field Development Manager, PDO**

The field of Knowledge Management has, for too long, remained under the radar screen. The enormous workplace changes taking place worldwide, as a result of the pandemic, provide this field a unique opportunity to shine, but it will require ongoing education. Most CEOs outside of certain fields don't even know what Knowledge Management does. This book adds to the important effort to educate the world about this critical field.

—Bruce Bolger, Founder- Enterprise Engagement Alliance

~ ~ ~

The book of Mr. Santhosh Shekar is a gap-filling guidance for knowledge managers and experts after the publication of the ISO 30401:2018 Knowledge Management System Requirements. The implementation of knowledge management "system" was/ is/will always be a big challenge for any organization. It is so complicated and connected to all activities of an organization, that nowadays not too many experts can overview the whole system.

I am a big fan and practitioner of Knowledge Management with more than 20 years of experience as Mr. Shekar. During my journey as a KM practitioner, I have helped many organizations to make the first steps in KMS establishment – at least tried! After issuing the ISO 30401:2018, the whole work has got a bit easier, but meanwhile challenges do surface. It shows how KM has to be aligned with other integrated standards, especially to ISO 9001:2015, the HR, training activities.

Mr. Shekar's book helps the readers understand the holistic picture. Besides, this book proves handy even for the experienced KM experts to implement and maintain their KM systems. If you are a beginner, it is recommended to read the introduction of the standard itself, the challenges, the advantage and the scope of KM. After understanding the context, you can start with the development phase described in Chapters 5-14. So, if you are already familiar with the context of the organization and understand where the knowledge can be found, you can go directly to Chapter 5.

This is another cookbook for KM Managers but not a simple one. Why? Because KM itself is connected to everything, it is a management tool, to help the management to make knowledgeable decisions. ... and decision-making is one of the most complicated and challenging processes.

One more important lesson: there are no unified solutions! You have to build up your KMS based on the ISO 30401:2015 requirements and international good practices. Mr. Shekar's book is a great support in it.

—Zoltan Pasztory; KM Consultant- Pasztory Consulting e.U

~ ~ ~

The ISO 30401 standard sets the requirements, scope and rules to be followed and provides guidelines for establishing, implementing, maintaining, reviewing and improving an effective management system for Knowledge Management in organizations. As an accredited ISO 30401 Auditor, Santhosh Shekar presents a comprehensive view on how managements can disseminate, share and develop their organization's knowledge assets. Santhosh identifies the challenges and advantages of implementing the ISO KM standard which will have a direct impact on the success of Knowledge Management at the organization. In order to implement and sustain KM using the ISO KM standard, Santhosh identifies ongoing evaluation and continuous improvement methods that will facilitate success. I would highly recommend this book as a valuable resource in establishing and/or standardizing the management of knowledge at your organization.

—Dr. Anthony J. Rhem, PhD., CEO/Principal Consultant-A.J. Rhem & Associates Inc. and Author of Knowledge Management in Practice

~ ~ ~

One of the prime reasons Knowledge Management has remained an enigma for many organizations is a dearth of awareness and expert guidance on how to go about it. Santhosh has done an admirable job through this book in demystifying KM and providing a step-by-step approach to set up a fully effective KM program within the organization, which is also fully compliant with the ISO 30401 standards. Icing on the cake is a treasure house of templates, checklists and tools in the appendices that could be applied as appropriate. The book fulfills a long-felt gap and I am confident it will help propel the KM journeys of organizations!

—Ved Prakash, CKO, Trianz

ACRONYMS

1. Org. – Organizations
2. KMS – Knowledge Management System
3. KM – Knowledge Management
4. KPI- Key Performance Indicator
5. KRA- Key Responsible Areas
6. MSME- Micro, Small, Medium Enterprises
7. ISO – International Organization for Standardization
8. KMP- Knowledge Management practices
9. KMSe- Knowledge Management Services
10. KMF- Knowledge Management Framework
11. KMT- Knowledge Management Technologies
12. MNC – Multi-National Companies
13. RACI- Responsible, Accountable, Consulted, Informed

PREFACE

I am writing this book for the novice in this field, those who are new to the knowledge management field, those who want to learn more about managing one's knowledge, those who are want to learn about the KM (Knowledge Management) Standard, those who are new to the KM standard. This book is a small effort to contribute towards creating awareness about Knowledge Management Standard and providing practical methods to implement the Knowledge Management System. In plain words, the knowledge shared in this book can easily be understood by the Non-IT and Non-Management audience. It is targeted for the audience from every walk of life. This book unleashes simple concepts and steps that can equip you to design your KMS (Knowledge Management System).

The book affirms the idea that one can design KMS based on the requirements, whether you are employed in a large MNC (Multinational Corporation), employed as a customer care executive, or whether you are a Project Manager in MSME (Micro, Small, Medium Enterprises) or a business leader leading strategic units. My experience, spanning over 20 years, has taught me that in any organization, the Management is responsible to run the organization, to make the business successful and from the employee's perspective pay the salaries on time. Of course, it is important for the management to focus on managing the knowledge area, but my concept and idea are exactly on a different tangent to this thought. I quote, "Anybody can execute knowledge management, whichever position you are in, whatever role you play, whether you are experienced or a rookie or whether you in an official capacity. You can even apply knowledge management in informal ways. This can help you immensely in enhancing the team's productivity, quality of business outcomes and you can work in collaboration with each other." This is how broad the spectrum of KM is.

KM, as a concept, is not just the responsibility of the management even if we view it from the lens of the traditional methodology. In this SMART world, KM is not just an approach but a necessity. The Digital transformation has empowered every knowledge worker[1] to manage their own knowledge effectively ever. So, undoubtedly and unfortunately, this is the most severe pandemic known to the current generation. However, in my opinion, this pandemic is a temporary phase (until everybody gets vaccinated). Therefore, as a knowledge worker, it is our responsibility to manage our own knowledge within the area of our work; and develop tenets to foster collaboration among fellow teammates. I always give prominence to the message that the managements, as such, do not have the bandwidth to cater to the knowledge-needs of every role in their organization. They may not even be aware of the degree of knowledge challenges at any particular layer of the organization. They have a set of goals and targets which have to be achieved.

These standards support successful, knowledge-driven and result-oriented strategies.

Whether you are a policymaker, or a KM student, or running a firm, business units, functions or the head of institutes; I am sure, you might be confronted with multiple challenges. A lot of energy and resources go into keeping the business afloat, bringing in the needed sales, converting the marketing funnel into winning clients, competitor's pressure, internal political distractions, managing capital, answering to managers, management, board and shareholders, answering to regulatory agencies.

Therefore, I have tried to orchestrate this book in a way wherein you can design your own KMS, no matter, wherever you are in the organization layer. While tailoring your own KMS, you can have a holistic view of practical problems faced by the organization, scoping your KM Outlook, developing KM Solution at the grass-root level, help KM Functions develop generic KM Frameworks and Toolkits, to walk you through a systematic way of KM Implementation aligned with the KM standard 30401.

Now, let me shine the torch on some of my prime achievements so far.

I have been an enthusiastic Knowledge Management practitioner during the course of the last two decades. I have spent significant time in every organization. I have worked in KM projects to understand the short-term and long-term KMS Lifecycle, its implications, pitfalls, winning strategies, engaging people at every level despite resistance. I have been a change-agent, generating significant cost-savings based on KM solutions, deriving value to business users, etc.

I have developed zero-cost Knowledge Management solutions in various organizations, which significantly led to multimillion-dollar additional businesses. I still stuck to my guns when better opportunities prevailed to switch from this profession. I persisted with this choice of working in the KM field, as it is one of the most dynamic blue-ocean emerging fields.

I have had also designed Knowledge Management architectures for Enterprises, Knowledge solutions for Business units, project-based lesson learned management systems, Learning knowledge management systems, Customer care - Product Knowledge bases, Managed Services based Knowledge Management systems, Knowledge Management systems for the Business Intelligence division. Some of my designs of KM systems have been working for over 10-12 long years and still going strong.

I also advise government and private organizations to establish KM functions and systems to manage the world after and during Pandemic events.

I have been a part of multiple Audit preparation teams representing KM areas during audits of ISO 9001, AutoSPICE Audit, ITIL (Information Technology Infrastructure Library) alignment of Managed Services. I have been an internal auditor for ISO 20000 Managed Services for several Managed services accounts.

This book answers all the questions about what is KM, what is not KM? How to start KM wherever you are? You can employ KM irrespective of the role you are playing and the company you might be working for. This book provides unique insights into invisible knowledge constraints which most of us have taken for granted and hence, we struggle every day in our work, personal life and other areas of life. The same applies to organizations, institutes, Government agencies and research/academia.

I can assure you that, once you have finished reading the book, you will be empowered to take actions in the most cluttered/challenging knowledge areas of your life/in your organizations and take actionable steps to enhance your experience of managing knowledge with high quality of knowledge visibility and enhanced collaboration.

If you can't distinguish the knowledge barriers and constraints around you, a different kind of frustration and stress pents-up in the area of work or the environment we work in. If only we could see the barriers and challenges from the knowledge domain, it would unveil how our performance gets affected by these knowledge barriers across the landscape of business.

I intend to share my learning experience, my insights into working with a number of customers, working in various circumstances and situations, wading through technological challenges, cruising through the people's behavior issues, rising above and beyond the barriers within and across the organization. I have succeeded in creating results in multiple organizations and I am sure, by end of this book, you will gain unique skill sets in managing your surrounding knowledge and drive effective results.

You will learn how to work with or without a budget, with a management sponsor or no official sponsor, manage your knowledge assets, become an expert, retain knowledge and get onboard with a certain degree of effectiveness.

Before I conclude the Preface, I would like to share what I have always heard from my teachers and I am sure even you might have heard this in your childhood. So, let me refresh your memory. There are three categories of people; the ones who make mistakes and continue to make the same mistakes all their lives, till it is too late to learn from those mistakes. Then the second category is the people who make mistakes once or twice, but learn quickly and do not repeat the mistakes. Last but not least, there is the third category of people who look at the first and second categories of people, they learn from other people's mistakes and experiences and do not repeat their mistakes. So this book is for the second and third category, who learn from themselves and others without shying away.

How to read this book? Chapters 1, 2 and 3 provide an overall understanding of the complexity of human interaction, knowledge constraints around oneself, KM basic, KM in other standard bodies, Introduction to ISO 30401 KMS standard.

Chapters 4, 5 and 7 provide an overview of how one can map the natural KM execution framework aligned to the ISO 30401 requirements. These chapters also highlight how one can plan/develop the KM toolkit and methodology for one's organization, with the practical case of marketing and sales as an example.

Chapters 8, 9, 10, 11 and 12 can be read independently, however, in each of the chapters, it is critical to understand the vastness and depth of KM lifecycle and its implementation in the organization.

Chapters 13 and 14 provide information about KPIs (Key Performance Indicators), Continuous Improvement and Audit Processes.

The book is supported by Appendix 1 to 5, which provides a 10-step guide to design KMS, a checklist of the questionnaire to develop KMS logically and systematically, along with mapping the Clauses and applicability.

CHAPTER ONE

INTRODUCTION TO KNOWLEDGE MANAGEMENT AND THE STANDARD

YES, this is how I remember the day when my colleagues started calling me an "E-MASTER!" I had designed a knowledge portal in the off-working hours during the initial phase of my career.

But what made me develop this portal? What made me come up with this idea?

Well, the answer is: it was a simple need of the hour!

Any technical/Non-Technical Customer Support center needs to address the customer query within a few seconds, or you have to resolve the technical issues by finding the root cause and solving it within strict timelines. The challenge was browsing through numerous manuals, websites and documents to find the right information. All I did was, I collated all the content needed from every source for every query and made it available online to the team in a most intuitive way. Within no time, all my colleagues started using it which became the second brain of the team and hence, I got the alias "E-master". That was how my journey started in the field of Knowledge management, even before I had heard the term Knowledge Management.

It all sprouted with a few simple questions......

"Why is it so difficult to find the information that I need to solve a query? Why can't I find all the needed information at one place?"

"Why is it so difficult for the organization to cater to my knowledge needs? Is the management aware of such challenges?"

Ever since those days to recent times, the challenges in the organizations are fundamentally the same and have only increased multifold with the sophistication of technology. The need remains the same, however, the questions keep changing in every role!

CONCEPT:

Let's start with the first important question; what is knowledge management?

1ST CONCEPT DEFINITION:

Knowledge management is an emerging management study that is in its toddler stage of evolution. Knowledge management in itself doesn't have one definition. Knowledge management is the ontological discipline i.e. every aspect of life, subject, topic will always be built on certain past knowledge and managing this conceptual knowledge in certain contexts is the essence of KM. This is more of a prerequisite especially in organizations and society to evolve into knowledge societies[2].

2ND CONCEPT DEFINITION:

Knowledge management is like Amoeba; a single living organism that doesn't have a definite shape. However, it does have certain boundaries and is finite.

Likewise, at this time, what we can define as knowledge management is very contextual and temporary for certain scope and time.

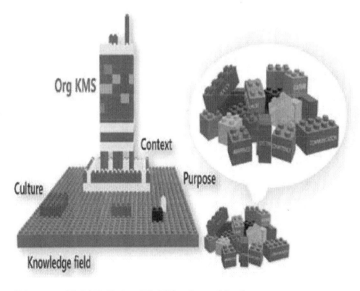

Diagram K.M.L.B 1 – KM like Lego blocks

However, in the case of knowledge management, it is not one specific discipline, it is an amalgamation of multiple fields, just like management, that covers the entirety of any subject matter, people and time. So, does KM follow a similar unchartered path?

In KM, we can't define KM in its entirety, however, we can define certain elements. Just like Lego Blocks, we can use various KM elements to build KM for any specific organization and individual needs.

HUMAN, CIVILIZATION, KNOWLEDGE FIELD

Knowledge emanates from the human mind and stretches far beyond time and space, hence the knowledge is both omnipresent and omnipotent, i.e. it is everywhere and at every place that the human mind perceives. The modern civilizations are built upon centuries of summation of knowledge and its application. This has given rise to cities, societies, civilizations, economies, discoveries and emerging fields in human lives.

Hence, it is important not to view knowledge management as a simple discipline, however, much different vocabulary is needed to describe it.

Knowledge and its management have grown with human development. The past, present; are all summations of the human's power of knowledge whether in the context of developing faiths, establishing societies, establishing laws of the land and human relationship. Knowledge permeates across different sections of human lives, into his livelihood, his survival instincts, and his abilities to advance in evolution.

Fundamentally, the human operates in the knowledge field, because of which all the subjects, fields, science, linguistics, behaviors, living systems, political systems, management systems; all are the integration of humankind's various past knowledge. Hence for me, knowledge management is not just a subject, not just a discipline, not just a profession, it is living and breathing in this domain like time and space. Knowledge has its properties, laws and mathematical models, which is going to branch out with the advent of computing and Artificial Intelligence.

The primary reason behind the human habitat evolving into kingdoms, colonies, countries, states, federal structure establishment was to enhance the equilibrium in the societies based on a certain time, past knowledge and belief systems. The living culture of humanities is the aftermath of past knowledge accumulated over centuries. Some part of this knowledge has been eroded, replaced with new knowledge that has been consciously added. Therefore, today's value system is largely determined by the old times and learning the economies.

Diagram H.E.O.K.F 1 –Human Evolution Operating on Knowledge Field

The evolution of humankind and various industries is cumulating the emergence of various knowledge cycles contributing to the present time. If we dwell on this evolution of societies and economies, we can very well say that humans have always operated in the field of knowledge. This is the field of knowledge that determines communication between other humans using language as tools, which developed into the written form of communication, which in turn spread the knowledge-flow much lucidly across the world.

According to early human histroy[3], in ancient times, the main occupation was hunting, gathering food in the forest and living in caves. With the invention of tools during the Stone Age, settlements started growing crops, and the barter system was established. The man entered into multifold development activities, learning new ways of transportation, agriculture irrigation system, fisheries, etc., it gave rise to various groups. These groups established their identities and from there on, small kingdoms were established. To protect their crops, properties and land, they had to raise armies and develop various armors and fighting tools. At the turn of every millennia or two, the man entered into New Age from Stone Age to Bronze Age, from Bronze Age to Metal Age and from Metal Age to Modern Era where kingdoms, colonies, countries evolved as the population increased. The competition gave way to wars which further fueled the rise of scientific research and the mass production era; the industrial revolution[4] started. And today, we are in a completely different form; the Era of Computing; which would lead to the Artificial Intelligence era sooner or later...

While in this process of evolution, a multitude of industries came into existence, giving rise to many more diverse industries and segments and it continues to evolve.

This macro scoping view of human evolution and understanding the field in which humans operate sets the background and context of what we are going to talk about; Knowledge Management. This book is a small step towards defining the attributes, boundaries and possibilities of the Knowledge Management field.

THE STANDARDS

The Importance of this standard is significant as it brings together critical elements of KM, the primary KM processes and key enablers to provide a common understanding within an organization and across the industries.

These common frameworks provide greater impetus to transparency, enhanced collaboration, amplifies the innovative spirit of enterprises, establishes the foundation of knowledge retention[5] and the management of intellectual capital[6]; both tangibles and intangibles.

Enterprises and corporations can further extend their commitment to the alliance with partner organizations, vendors, suppliers, customers, clients, regulators, agencies and government bodies. They can embed the KM principles in designing the knowledge management practices in areas of collaboration practices, asset management practices, KM technologies[7] practices, Enterprise Content/Records Management practices, Intellectual Capital management, enhancing human capital performance and engagement practices. These areas are very broad and will continue to grow.

Example: In a different context, when the allopathy[8] field emerged during the 17th century, the inquisitiveness of finding the human body function and organs created a new field of medical practitioners like doctors and nurses. However, over the period of time, today, there are wide fields developed in every organ of human beings like pulmonary, vision, teeth, urinary, gynecology, psychology and so on. Even though humans as a whole need to be healed, yet the focus areas and specialty areas have emerged over decades of medical field development.

Similarly, in the organizations before the ISO 9001[9] standard (International Standard for a Quality Management System) and the introduction of computers, the design of the corporation was available only in these quality management documents. For anybody who wanted to understand the mechanism, these documents would provide the entire working of the organization, processes involved and people responsible, whether producing goods or providing services could be determined. Earlier, the total quality management movement and most of the organization's entire working were driven by few people like the proprietor or the supervisor and to some extent the foreman. At that time, the movement of people between organizations was very low and employees would work for organizations till their retirement. Hence, knowledge loss was practically zero or nil. As the economies around the world developed, new products and services gave way to new jobs, this expansion of jobs steadily raised the opportunities for employment and slow movement transpired before the computing era.

With the passage of time, large organizations realized these challenges with smaller firms that were providing auxiliary materials and parts. Therefore, these large organizations started supplying various materials that would gain value with a quality management system. This documentation of the working of the organizations, their processes and work products offered services that created the first organizational explicit knowledge base. These standards captured the essence of organizational processes, people and information about the functions. The small and medium organizations got a new benchmarking method to put things in place which could provide USP in the marketplace, creating robustness in managing their processes and documenting them became an essential step.

These were the seedlings of the first knowledge asset management in organizations that were purely dependent on physical papers, folders and files to document the essential requirements. With the advent of computing and the world wide web, the dynamics of the organization changed; it revolutionized the working of organizations, enterprises and started utilizing computers to store and manage data. It also created a need to share content from one computer to another, which gave way to the intranet, which in turn gave way to an evolution of a large network of systems i.e. network operating systems. The network operating systems paved way for connectivity between different locations. This was upgraded to multiple networks of large connection of systems. And this worldwide web has transformed this big blue marble into a global village.

As you see, the entire computing technology gave rise to a new way of sharing, collaborating and generating an opportunity for individuals, groups and organizations to share information and data. Humans have been successful in creating computer systems, network systems and collaboration systems. But what about the human part i.e. the psychological, emotional and physical? Have we evolved as much as it is required in organizations? Or have we learned to manage our fears, anxiety, uncertainty, insecurity in a certain environment and share and collaborate with one another in a certain context?

Unfortunately, the answer to the above questions is; to a very limited extent.

Then what's the solution?

Knowledge Management.

ISO 30401 KMS:2018 standard has anchored this field very firmly, from here on it's our responsibility to develop this field into an essential field of study in academics/research and critical functions in Organizations/Societies/Institutes.

Knowledge Management has been mentioned in various standards, industry's best practices, and frameworks. Few are listed below:

1. Automotive SPICE® Process Reference Model Process Assessment Model
2. Telecom TL9001 – KM requirements
3. ISO 9001 – Organizational Knowledge
4. eSCM-SP (e-Sourcing Capability Model for Client Organizations) V2 - KM Requirements
5. ISO 55001 Asset management — Management systems — Requirements

6. ISO 15489-1 Information and documentation — Records management -General

7. CMMI® – CAPABILITY MATURITY MODEL® INTEGRATION – Organizational Training

8. ISO-44001 Collaborative Business Relationship Management Framework

BS ISO 56002:2019 Innovation management — Innovation management system — Guidance

This standard; 7.1.4 Knowledge speaks about how an organization should effectively manage knowledge as a pre-requisite for innovation management.

Automotive SPICE® Process Reference Model Process Assessment Model

In Automotive SPICE, the clauses 4.8 Reuse Process Group, REU.2 Reuse Program Management and 8.3 RIN.3 Knowledge Management Clause talk about the requirement of reuse initiative and KM systems for organizations based on the industrial requirements.

Enhanced Telecom Operations Map (eTOM)– The business process framework for Knowledge and Research management:

KNOWLEDGE & RESEARCH MANAGEMENT PROCESSES

| KNOWLEDGE | RESEARCH | TECHNOLOGY |
| MANAGEMENT | MANAGEMENT | SCANNING |

Courtesy: Amdocs.com/public/etom6.pdf | eTOM 6.0 Poster Design

This enterprise management process grouping focuses on knowledge management, technology research within the enterprise and evaluation of potential technology acquisitions.

ITIL V3 PROCESS MODEL

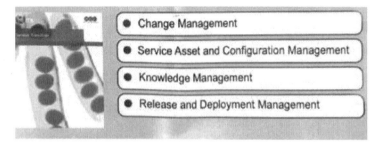

Image Courtesy: ilx group plc http:ilxgroup.com

ESCM-SP STANDARD

The eSourcing Capability Model for client organization (eSCM-CL) v1.1

In this model, there is a specific clause on how to manage client knowledge management as one of the capability areas, it talks about effective KM practices with regard to sharing knowledge, providing required resources, reuse knowledge, etc.

My primary intention behind inking this book is to create one, yet, result-driven KM Manual or guide across the spectrum for the audience, industry/segment categories, novice or experts, KM leadership, ones who have just started or are already in the KM journey, academic interest or practitioners. Applying these KM philosophies can catalyze impactful results.

This book is a humble effort to contribute in some way to the evolution of this majestic, everlasting and ever-growing field called "Knowledge Management".

The book identifies such human-centric challenges.

ISO 30401: 2018 KMS

The Diagram K.M.S.F.D[10] of ISO 30401 Clause is arranged in Plan Do Check Act Cycle [8] – to provide an overview of the KM requirements. The standard doesn't provide any solution but a contextual reference in terms of requirements for the knowledge entity.

The book unfurls a functional model for ISO 30401 requirements and dwells deep into each of the requirements and possible solutions. My motive is to aid organizations and individuals who can refer to a body of knowledge to establish KM, kick-start KM, prepare for Certification, develop KM systems that are effective, view KM practices as a discipline, provide a glimpse of the breadth and width of KM field and its enormous benefits.

In the era of the knowledge-based economy, an organization needs to create a knowledge management framework. The ISO 30401 KMS is an internationally established knowledge management framework. This book has been crafted to assist an organization to structure its implementation on the ISO 30401 standard based on some good practices based on my 20 years of experience as a KM practitioner. Through this book, I aspire to provide a practical and systematic way of designing the KM system in enterprises and corporations.

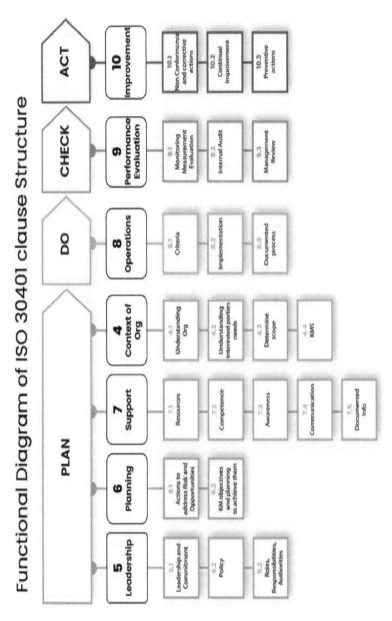

Diagram K.M.S.F.D. – KMS Functional Diagram of ISO 30401

This book offers possibilities of different flavors of KM approaches, implementation methodology, design techniques and concepts to assist you in developing KMS that are compliant with ISO standard requirements.

My focus is to increase awareness and knowledge on how KMS could be implemented effectively in any knowledge entity or body; such that other standard aspects like documentation and evidence are by-products of the KM work.

To Design effective KMS is to:

- Address the knowledge needs and fill the gaps of the organization holistically

- Enhance the creation/visibility/accessibility of knowledge and reuse of it

- Effectively increase collaboration, communication, knowledge exchange among people

- Manage the compliance of standard effectively

The standard could be interpreted in infinite possibilities and I don't claim this to be the only truth. The concepts and models presented in this book are one of such possibilities, which I think can provide insight into the complexities of organizational KM, the width and depth of KM practices and a generic way of doing things.

This book has been engineered to assist an organization to structure its implementation on ISO 30401 standard based on some good practices

The book encompasses two aspects:

1. Generic interpretations of the standard

2. How to go about designing the KMS for your organization

After reading this book, you will find an increase in your awareness and knowledge of how KMS could be implemented effectively in a knowledge entity or body.

You may find many books on the shelf that talk about KM. However, this book presents my experiences condensed into simple and practical steps to provide the complete set of KM methods, models, framework, system architecture, etc. I have tried to cover KMS in its entirety whether it's at the project level or organizational level, whether you want to break into small pieces and address with KM or solve organization Knowledge needs holistically. The book scales the field and boundary to the next level, creating a common sense of perception on what KM is, how KM systems work, how the KM framework needs to be designed, how KM solutions can be designed, how KM functions and operates, etc. It also helps and supports to organize and establish working KM function.

If the standard is at a generic level, the book becomes specific to each and every requirement and examines various options on how it could be implemented. There are various tools and models illustrated for KM practice benefits. These concepts, models, frameworks and body of knowledge are my own creation and reproduction to enhance the practical, theoretical understanding of the interested audience. I would say, these are some of the best practices contextualized at a level where practitioners or interested parties can find new meaning and put various questions and answers in certain contexts.

The ISO recommends what you document, you do; and what you do, you document. The three primary requirements of the standard are:

1. Effectiveness of Knowledge Management Systems

2. Documentation

3. Evidence

It is said that the organization or the knowledge entity should be prepared to showcase the effectiveness of the knowledge management, i.e. if it is making a difference to the business or the interested party's defined problem and solving using the various KM system. Can you show the evidence for the same? So, what you do and what is documented are the same?

These are the fundamental needs to comply with the standard.

The book aims at creating awareness about designing KMS for the audience like business leaders, KM students and managers to understand the primary essence. You can fathom the vastness and depth of this field and choose certain tools and methods to implement in your organization to make a difference.

CHAPTER TWO

UNIVERSAL KNOWLEDGE MANAGEMENT CHALLENGES

There are innumerous ways to interpret the standard and develop KMS. Even before looking at knowledge management solutions, one has to understand the underlying nature of knowledge entities.

The knowledge models are what aid the organizations and individuals to build their capability and eventuate a continuous journey of improvement in the field of Knowledge-Based Economy[11]. Therefore, the organization should be well-grounded to listen to the market, emerging and disruptive wave of changes, adapting and evolving to these impulses. The organization must be aligned and agile to form and reform organizational teams to cater to the need of a specific cause that is very important.

There should be clear visibility of knowledge flow[12] in the organizations, highly visible knowledge interfaces and high conducive knowledge marketplace within and across the organization. This is what can enable healthy knowledge development, management and innovation.

The standard way of doing things will help the organization to deliver results in a much-accelerated way and focus on the effectiveness of the KMS.

KNOWLEDGE FLOW

Generally, what we see in the organization chart[13] and the structure of the organization is how we typically emulate when we think of knowledge flow too.

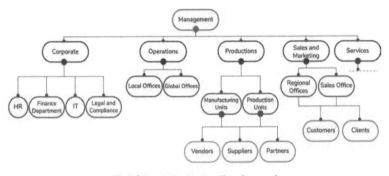

Typical Organization Structure-Flow of command

Diagram T.O.K.F 1 – Traditional Organizational Knowledge Flow

However, the knowledge flow is more complex and has no hierarchy in reality. For example: The knowledge needed to repair a vehicle is independent of the MD of the Service Center. Similarly, a salesperson can sell the most expensive product with the least effort, however, it is independent of the creator of the product or the execution of knowledge. There is something else at play in every working organization:

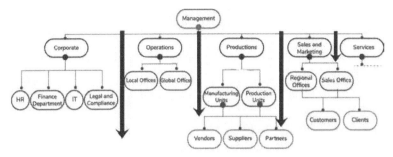

Typical Organization Knowledge-Flow perception

Diagram T.O.K.F 2 – Traditional Organizational Knowledge Flow

The next diagram depicts how we see the knowledge flow happening in the organization in real-time and pretty much constant at any point in time. They cut across the boundaries of functions/service lines/offices, etc.

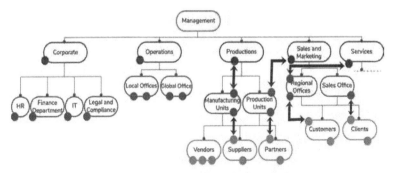

If we map them, then we can derive a Organizational Knowledge Matrix

Diagram A.O.K.F 1 – Actual Organizational Knowledge Flow

Organizational Knowledge Matrix[14]- It represents the exact blueprint of the organizational knowledge flow, knowledge barriers, knowledge entities. Hence, it is important to understand the organizational knowledge flow or the value stream of knowledge flow within and across the boundaries of the organization. This is also the first step in defining your requirements for interested parties.

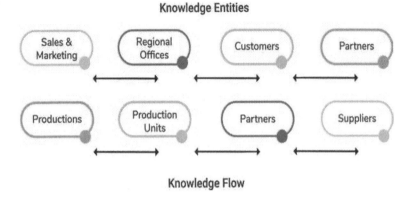

Diagram O.K.M. 1 – Organizational Knowledge Matrix

Having laid out this matrix will help the organization in understanding the knowledge gluts, clogs, barriers, highly used knowledge bodies, lowly used knowledge bodies, etc.

Based on the population size and highly used knowledge bodies, it is essential to develop and set up the scope of KMS.

In the above organizational diagram T.O.K.F 1 and diagram T.O.K.F 2, the knowledge flows are top to down. The flow of knowledge in a traditional hierarchical organization can have various challenges with greater barriers between functions and other knowledge entities.

The flow of knowledge is very complicated in a matrix organization. However, in the matrix, although the flow happens across the organization, but it is staged and scattered in its nature. Hence, it becomes important that the organization realizes these flows of knowledge to create incredible "resilience".

What does resilience in the nature of entity means? An organization is considered resilient when it's aware and sensitive to its environment and demand, when it is willing to adapt and change to generate better results by reinventing its internal knowledge processes and developing the required body of knowledge.

The organizations are formed with people coming together to achieve a common goal and objective by catering to the needs and demands of the market either through services or products or allied services. So we need to examine the fundamental unit i.e. Knowledge worker's role in the organization and how it imparts resilience and agility to the organization. Such conditions are extrapolated with multiplied factors of various Knowledge layers, innumerable knowledge entities, and order - Knowledge needs to understand the underlying forces, dynamics and pitfalls to make the KMS succeed.

HUMAN AS KNOWLEDGE ENTITY

Every transaction starts with human thinking, especially in the context of knowledge flow and knowledge source; it is essential for us to understand that every action starts with the individual mind.

A need to process, a need for information, a need to speak, a need to ask, a need to search, a need to find, of course, the reason beyond these needs vary with context, situation and circumstances that occur in one's mind. In the Diagram H.K.E.1- Human as knowledge entity -Self constraints model represents the construct of the average human mind. These barriers affect each individual in different ways, shaping and altering one's experience. It also reveals how one reacts or behaves when a certain environment varies.

Diagram H.K.E.1 – Human as Knowledge Entity – Self-Constraints

Some of the factors can be restrictive or supportive in human transactions. They are:

- Perceptual constraints[15]
- Auditory constraints
- Mental/Mind processing constraints
- Experiential constraints
- Psychological constraints

These factors impact the everyday working in an organization:

1. **Perceptual constraints** – What we see, do or perceive is always based on our preconceived notion of matters; It could also be given by various domains where we can't perceive beyond what we feel, hear and experience.

2. **Auditory constraints** – are always limited to how much we hear (get the intention of the speaker/need/ wants, etc.), to understand or how much do we really listen to what people ask?

3. **Mind/mental constraints**- What challenges arise to understand a new subject, faculties to solve problems in different fields, areas, processes, information are beyond our own known knowledge. What is our memory capacity and power to retain information and knowledge; and store the information within our lives, organization and careers?

4. **Experiential knowledge:** This knowledge is acquired only through practice and experience like swimming or floating, cycle balance, etc., these can be gained through practice. So certain knowledge can be acquired only through practice and going through certain actions and situations over a period of time (practice).

5. **Psychological constraints:** Our deep embedded desires, characteristics, nature plays a big role in our transaction world, it elevates our exchange or disempowers in our transactions. Ex: Being angry and brooding all the time, will invoke a different response from the team members;

As we have seen above, these are the first set of knowledge challenges at the individual level which can impair the overall network of the organization's hierarchy and responsiveness and/or if addressed, can actually amplify resilience in the organization with greater individual responsiveness.

SPECTRUM OF KNOWLEDGE INTERFACE

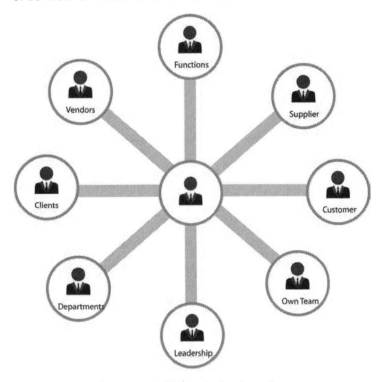

Spectrum of Knowledge Interface

Diagram S.O.K 1 – Spectrum of Knowledge Interface

The Spectrum of Knowledge[16] (Diagram S.O.K 1) interface illustrates how an employee interacts with multiple stakeholders within and outside the organization to achieve the organization's objectives and personal key performance indicators.

As you see, the spectrum of knowledge interface is limited in certain roles, however, the same spectrum increases multifold.

Also, the employee lifecycle in the organization determines this spectrum. As the employee grows in the organizational hierarchies, the spectrum keeps expanding to include every function, department, customer, internal and external knowledge entities.

Diagram S.O.K. 2 shows that the context of the knowledge interface spectrum may increase based on the activity and task. A software professional who is looking to gain finesse in coding may need to just interface with few roles; however, if you work in shared services, you would be interacting with innumerable people, so on and so forth.

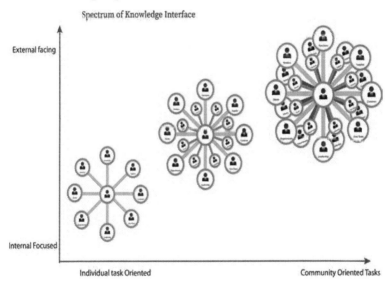

Diagram S.O.K. 2 – Spectrum of Knowledge Interface

So, when one individual communicates with another in the work environment, there are multiple constraints acting upon in this point-to-point communication.

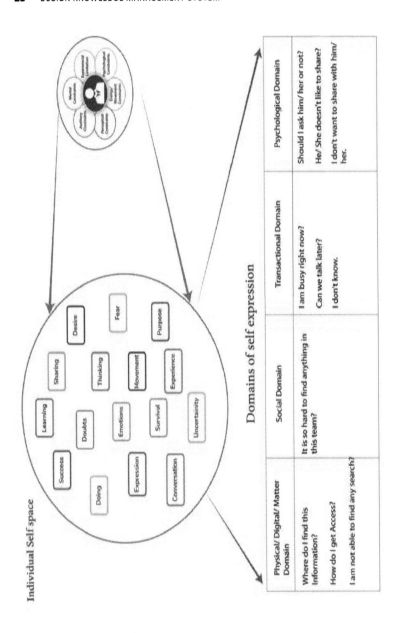

Diagram I.D.S.E 1 – Individual Domain of Self Expression

In the computing and mobile world; communication happens with certain common TCP/IP protocol conformance, hardware supporting them, and the driver's ability to send and receive exact data between each other. Hence the communication and digital content exchange between any two computing devices are almost the same.

However, when it comes to information exchange between two individuals, it is never straight forward. The Diagram I.D.S.E 1 – Individual Domain of Self Expression Model, represents different states of human mind thought patterns; either or all of which will yield certain results, or create friction, or create thought overflows, or can also create frustrations.

Example: As a new member in a team, if you need to find out about certain ways of doing things or taking cue on decision criteria:

1. You start with a question in your mind. (with all the constraints given by one's human potential, which is influenced by the barriers) and find yourself with no answer or need more details.

2. The next natural step is to reach out to your colleagues sitting around you or pick a phone to call somebody in the organization or a person whom you report to or reaching out to somebody who is having authority on that particular subject.

3. When you ask you might get a positive response; or various other kinds of responses, where your value proposition before and after asking the questions remains the same, but you might think otherwise.

4. When these experiences accumulate over a period of time for anyone or many individuals; when they encounter any hardship, they would hesitate to ask, or it becomes a major barrier to ask somebody who could help; as either the expert is too busy, there is no sufficient documentation or there is no sufficient guidance, etc.

In the Diagram I.D.S.E 1 - Individual Domain of Self Expression, this model of inter-domain conversations occurs within one's mind, what you actually hear and what you actually speak in the group and the kind of thoughts that surface while dealing with the digital domain is an example. The spectrum of conversations can vary from one individual to another depending upon one's innate nature. Human understanding, human memory capacity, human's life capacity to manage time, human's wisdom to leading a life; all affect an individual while at work; apart from skills, competency, experience and mindset. To add, human understanding, comprehension, sensitivity, responsiveness, activeness and dynamics differ from individual to individual.

What we saw was a simple scenario in one situation of an individual mind. However, in the organization, the gravity and degree of an individual's desire to succeed, achieve and prove oneself impact others in different ways; similarly, the fear of losing, failure and surviving inducts different sets of emotions and conversations in one's mind. These create different actions that are predictable and unpredictable which would have a social impact.

Knowledge Flow between two Knowledge entities

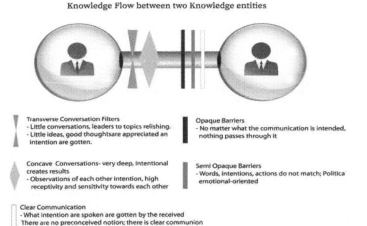

! Transverse Conversation Filters
   - Little conversations, leaders to topics relishing.
   - Little ideas, good thoughtsare appreciated an
     intention are gotten.

◆ Concave Conversations- very deep, intentional
   creates results
   - Observations of each other intention, high
     receptivity and sensitivity towards each other

▌ Opaque Barriers
   - No matter what the communication is intended,
     nothing passes through it

▌ Semi Opaque Barriers
   - Words, intentions, actions do not match; Politica
     emotional-oriented

   Clear Communication
   - What intention are spoken are gotten by the received
   There are no preconceived notion; there is clear communion
   between the two individuals or knowledge entity

Diagram K.E.K.E.1 – Knowledge Flow between two Knowledge Entities

At the next social level, the knowledge exchange happening between two humans has the possibility of the following categories of knowledge flow or exchange.

1. Clear Knowledge Flow- The intent behind the spoken words can be comprehended by the receiver and vice versa, these are the regular communications within the teams and organizations.

2. Transverse Knowledge Flow- Contextual conversation, the intention is to create awareness, commanding, teaching and expanding knowledge horizons. The flow of such conversations is top-down, for example, the leads asking team members to work on an assignment, etc.

3. Concave Knowledge Flow– This knowledge flow is very deep, highly intentional; creates results, observations

of each other's intention, highly receptive and sensitive towards each other. This could be through conversations in Focused groups, workshops, peer assist groups, outcome-based meetings.

4. Semi-Opaque Knowledge Flow- Depends on the mood and emotions of the person to receive or share knowledge; the intentions are different, words could be different at different times/situations.

5. Opaque Barriers- No Knowledge flows; no matter what the situation is, the knowledge flow is absent; Intentions are clear, Hostile environment.

WORLD OF KNOWLEDGE CONSTRAINTS

If we have to view the world from the knowledge domain, considering everything one sees and experiences, we can infer to the point of reference. This point is associated with knowledge sources[17] or knowledge bodies as a whole in which one operates, the world of humans and various forms of human societies. This also includes everything man-made whether in physical, electronic, computing/digital form, AI-world and everything nature has created including living and non-living that forms the finite knowledge sources. This becomes the epitome, epicenters where knowledge, information, and data are being exchanged to build a civilization and sustain nature.

The entities listed below provide holistic knowledge about Entities Matrix:

1. Individual Knowledge Entities – are the humans as knowledge source -experts, conversations, teaching,

questions, actions, etc. This has been already covered in the earlier section.

2. Man-Made Knowledge Entities – All knowledge sources which have been created by humans whether Digital world, Computing world, Electronic world, Physical world, etc.

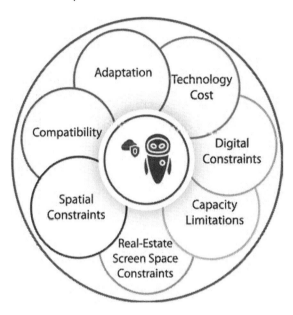

Diagram. K.E.D.M 1 – Knowledge Electronics/Digital Medium Constraints

3. Societal Knowledge Entities – are the various elements constituting political dynamics, survival/competitive markets, social belief systems, religion, etc. as the knowledge source.

4. Natural Knowledge Entities – are the sources of knowledge whether its galaxy, natural environment-

water, hills, lands, ocean, animals, organism, human as species, etc.

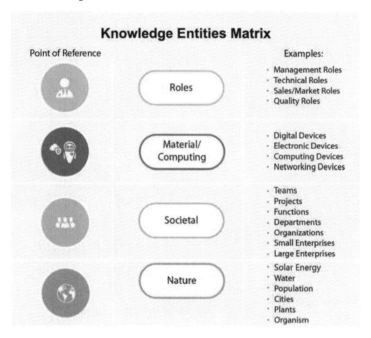

Diagram K.E.M.1 – Knowledge Entities Matrix

The world of knowledge constraints is one of the representations of the constraints across the ecosystem, multiplied into the knowledge entities, Natural Knowledge entities, Individual knowledge Worker, Societal knowledge entities. Each of these represents multiple domains of the sources of knowledge, each having its own nature, properties and attributes in this transactional world. It is essential to get a bird's-eye-view of this dimension before moving forward. Please refer to the Diagram W.o.K.C 1 – World of Knowledge Constraints. The representation of this model is critical for one's understanding even before making the journey to develop knowledge management solutions. Do we see the world as it is and understand the unseen drivers in the organization, complexities under which one operates, complexities between individuals, the environment in which one operates, things that are affecting one's performance or team's performance, etc. To dwell deep into this model is not the aim of this book. It provides a basic introduction.

This vision helps us gain insight into the problem at hand and the magnanimity of challenges when it comes to knowledge exchange i.e. managing something so dynamic, so unpredictable, ever-changing, state of the knowledge entities and bodies.

The world view given here represents an individual's view and how he interacts with the material world, groups/teams/societies, how he interacts with other individuals, how he interacts with the world/nature/time, etc.

Once we have the individual constraints, it can be extrapolated to every next point we are focusing on or interacting with.

Ex: A sales manager interacting with the market, his own team members, leadership team, technologies, devices. Vendors, clients, etc. The knowledge needed in his span of knowledge interface is humanoid, hence it is completely different from a customer support engineer.

How does an individual experience Digital World, Physical World, Natural World, Society/Organizations?

How does an individual experience World Experiencing Organizations?

How does an individual experience World Experiencing Digital, Electronic, Material world?

How does an Individual interact with other individuals? How does the 2nd order of experiencing the world occur? How is the 2nd order of Digital, Physical, Material and Natural world experienced through other individuals?

When the first step on the moon is experienced by the man, that is what is experienced by the world.

When Global warming is experienced by the affected people, how does the world or human societies respond to it?

The knowledge of self-constraints and control over one's greed, anger, lust, pride, are essential to create social harmony. In the transactional world, the spark of all action starts with man's psychological work in the mind- the desire. Managing their knowledge becomes essential in order to respect and serve the natural order in the physical world. As we know and have, experienced when one doesn't have sustainable development in the mind, that would influence policymaking at the highest level of nations, world bodies and other groups that are looking at world peace, prosperity and human goodness.

The above model basically puts a different perspective of the multitude of the world we live in as one, yet one world is impacting the other in major ways.

The important message, the knowledge which our generation needs to manage is the knowledge at self-level, this would be essential for world peace and prosperity among humans.

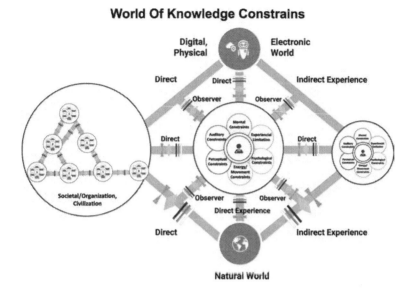

Diagram W.o.K.C 1 – World of Knowledge Constraints

Though we are looking at knowledge management in a single dimension, but if we apply the above model, it helps us to scope our knowledge management towards greater benefits of knowledge, economics, knowledge nations and society being responsible for oneself. It can also help in other's living and living with others; being sensitive for other's living is the greatest of all knowledge- sustainable development, sensitive and responsible human living.

CHAPTER THREE

ADVANTAGES OF KNOWLEDGE MANAGEMENT SYSTEMS

ORGANIZATIONAL LEARNING

KNOWLEDGE – THE KEY TO SUCCESS

- Successful companies can lose their market share as a new company comes out with services and products that can challenge the existing line of products.

- Their competition in the economy is always driven by the superiority of quality and market demand. A company can steer ahead of the competition curve, leveraging on its organization's knowledge.

- An organization's knowledge is dependent on how well the people in the organization can utilize the past, present knowledge to create a prosperous future.

- Organizational life cycles[18] are finite. Therefore, if the organization does not adapt to the new wave of market, demand and future technologies, it will perish. And the underlying determent factor is always the knowledge field on which they operate.

If you look at the industrial revolution and the modern information age[19], you will find that some organizations have survived for over centuries, some few decades and some few years.

Similarly, every time humanity discovers a new field of economy, it opens up infinite possibilities. During the 14th century when European continents discovered a new sea route to the edge of the world, this knowledge changed the global geopolitics. New colonization[20] emerged, as that declined after 2 centuries, new capitalism and globalization flattened the globe. This again provided knowledge transfer and learning for countries, to emerge in the new modern times to challenge the old order.

Therefore, the uniqueness of knowledge, whether it is an organization or societies or nations can lead to the rise and fall of nations.

Hence, knowledge innovation, transfer, application and protection are very critical for one's existence at every level of knowledge entities.

The organization can make a difference when the intellectual capital i.e. the people working for the organization work together to achieve a common goal. This common goal could be to make the organization the best in terms of greater quality, right pricing, catering to the right audience, doing everything based-on the market demand while innovating.

In teams and between departments, there are always tendencies to compete within to raise in position, for which the heads and managers in the top and middle management create dynamics, sometimes excelling the organization process or curbing the development functions, departments.

Their interpersonal dynamics create a huge rift in the working relationship between teams, create redundancy due to miscommunication, thwarted communication and mis-coordination. This acts as one of the major barriers between teams.

There are times when there is a need to share certain insights from the market sales or employees who are in touch with the organization. They can't communicate and coordinate if there is no mechanism of collaboration established in the organization.

The barriers between people-to-people within the team not sharing insights to their superiority, between departments, between functions are some of the greater factors that hamper the organization's growth. These factors eventually decay the organization within, affecting the organization's resilience to adapt.

Aspects like skilling, reskilling, training and mentoring the employees on different challenges contribute to the individual's performance and expertise level. If these aspects are designed based on the organization's requirements, then it can help the organization grow at an accelerated pace.

Today, an individual's attitude, preference and motivation to skill and reskill depend on the following psychological constituents:

- Some workers are highly self-motivated.
- Some workers need some support.
- Some workers need a push.

But some, even after all the support is provided, aren't inclined to learn and reskill their knowledge.

The other aspect of individual learning is how well the organization is training an individual to support his learning needs and project needs.

There are multiple barriers for an individual to be effective in his duties. These knowledge challenges affect the organization's overall capability.

KNOWLEDGE ECONOMY

Knowledge work is increasingly important in many societies and organizations; many economies aspire to become knowledge economies, where knowledge is the main source of wealth.

What is knowledge work?

What is knowledge economy?

How societies and organizations can leverage knowledge?

We have to talk a bit about world history, to understand the larger context of the knowledge economy.

Human civilization started with hunting, animal husbandry, agriculture, mining, trading as the most fundamental economic activities forming cities, towns and determining the course of nations.

With man learning navigation[23], this knowledge opened new routes to new continents and new ways of trade. Colonies were born, the new source created new prosperity and led to the industrial revolution. Man, production and machinery knowledge changed the landscape of societies, displacing, older economies and giving raise to large scale production, the genesis of modern-day business management[24] , a new field were born.

With the knowledge, innovations[25], steam engine, railways, electricity, telephony, computer, internet, mobility, AI have had major implications in the societies. Managing their field of new knowledge has led the organizations and nations to prosper and every time, a new knowledge economy has been raised. It is today that societies are not just doing agriculture, mining, oil and gas, timber or other basic earth-based economies.

The knowledge economy enthralls the intellectual utilization of human as a resource to support, create and develop new products, services and innovative ideas which will lead to the transformation of societies in every century; the human societies learn these important aspects, adopt and start dominating the world. Hence, every nation needs to embrace the management of their traditional, cultural, industrial and economic knowledge to shape the new knowledge economy, which would alter the fundamental shift in global power over the next few decades.

ORGANIZATION AND INDIVIDUAL

The average working cycle of individuals[26] is about 30-35 years and the learning curves take multiple elevations based on the change in roles, responsibilities, company, the field of employment, etc. If we consider from an organization's perspective, it is imperative that the employee who joins becomes productive as early as joining the organization.

Some of the key challenges we must consider here for our organizations are::

- Hiring experienced employees costs more to the company.
- Hiring experienced employees costs more to the client who may not be willing to pay.
- Company needs to hire freshers from the market and provide them training and real-time learnings to make them productive, which costs money.

At another level, employees keep moving to different roles within the organization, their movements again require knowledge for the new roles, who are taking up the roles. Again, there are bigger challenges in the organization; job rotation and promotions are displacing a lot of knowledge experts, creating a vacuum when they move out of their respective role to take up a higher or lateral position.

The other challenges are employees moving out of companies, creating greater knowledge erosion from where they move out.

Then there are individuals who are self-motivated to move up the ladder, they become specialists in their domain. There is competition within to upskill and grow in the organizational ladder, skill and competency level.

Then there are staff who want to continue on the status quo, till something major impacts their career or job.

The company can benefit only if it on boards various roles by cutting down learning cycles, upskills existing employees, retains employee's knowledge using multiple learning strategies, practices to develop in-depth skills and competency and provides access to experts to exchange their ideas and experience with others.

This will certainly provide increased access to knowledge. Again, knowledge is contextual to this role and individual/organizational aspirations are based on the organization's context that makes the learning culture a natural way of working.

DYNAMIC ORGANIZATIONS AND EMPLOYEE TURNOVER

In today's knowledge economy, the importance of knowledge creation, consolidation, application and reuse is very important. In the previous topic, we learned about, staff movements in an organization that leads to a knowledge vacuum. This vacuum creates knowledge erosion[27] in the organizations. Hence, it is necessary to develop a knowledge infrastructure around every role in the organization.

Every organization provides Physical infrastructure to an employee, like laptop, chairs, Pedestal, Digital Infrastructure like Network access, Email account, etc. in the current/post-Corona time. During the Pandemic, the organizations are just onboarding employees, sending a laptop.

The organization needs to take initiatives to develop a Knowledge Infrastructure[28], where every role in the organization can get relevant information, Knowledge, Contacts, Artifacts, Know how, processes, Technical, or Domain, skills and competency development, work task flows; like assembly lines in production era.

The important question is, how can the knowledge infrastructure be provided to the employees? How can employers create a knowledge infrastructure that makes onboarding, technical, domain, process, networking fetch all the knowledge at the click of a button, high collaborative online environment, highly visible knowledge systems, etc.?

The Circle of Knowledge–role-based Model represents the idea of how role-based complex knowledge infrastructure is the need of the hour, which emulates all the requirements for a role and complete knowledge lifecycles[29] are designed. The example of software engineer -Circle of knowledge clearly shows the requirements when it comes to day-to-day productivity, operations, learning and performance of a role.

Diagram C.o.K 1 - Circle of Knowledge

Similarly, the Circle of Knowledge- team-based is required at the function or project level as a team collaboration and inter-collaboration infrastructure. If the team works on shared services and in the matrix organization, the circle of knowledge differs. An example has been provided in the Circle of Knowledge-Functions/project/department – interactions. The circle of knowledge for the marketing team may be regarding the formulation of policies, case studies, procedures, templates; all should be easily available and printable when needed.

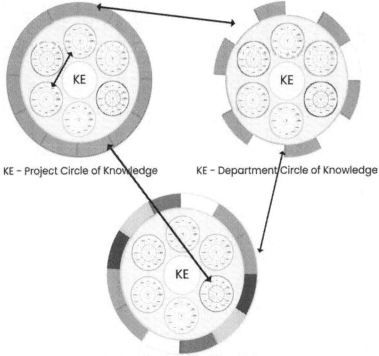

KE – Project Circle of Knowledge

KE – Department Circle of Knowledge

KE – Functional Circle of Knowledge

Diagram C.o.K 2 Circle of Knowledge-Functions/Project/ Department

The basic documentation management is done in an ad-hoc fashion, hence the organization needs to take a pro-active role to identify and develop the necessary knowledge associates circle of knowledge. Similarly, every Technocrat works with his circle of knowledge, Business Leaders work with their circle of knowledge, so on and so forth. For every role across the organization, Functional roles have a circle of knowledge, departmental roles have a circle of knowledge, similarly whether its private or government organizations, every role on this planet have their circle of knowledge:

The organization needs to acknowledge and establish this invisible Knowledge infrastructure and should address it using the Knowledge management philosophy to counter knowledge erosions.

KNOWLEDGE, EVOLUTION AND KNOWLEDGE EXCHANGE

During the 18th century, machines were invented[30] to do the same job or product over a number of times so as to save time.

If one mason created an artifact in one day, they came out with molds, which could create similar kinds of products much quicker. Similarly, the molds, pulleys, logs, engines were all the mechanisms to increase the productivity of various activities and this kept evolving. Industrial production, assembly lines with human intervention got replaced with AI assemble lines.

Similarly, products development[31] have been streamlined, agriculture has been industrialized[32], computing has been introduced, software has streamlined the business processes and works. Now, the next wave is digital transformation, IoT,

Cloud Computing, AI, etc. where intellectual capital forms the backbone of the latest revolutionary phase.

This leads to an important question, how to organize knowledge that is reusable, and how can it be made easily available and facilitate the digital transformation?

If you are a software engineer, what is your circle of knowledge? Refer to diagram C.o.K.1 as an example, the circle of knowledge needs can expand to finite series; however, with digital knowledge, it is humanely impossible to use one's human memory.

The circle of knowledge can be applied to any knowledge role and knowledge organization. Training, Competency building, Technology centers, Management classes, Leadership phases should be made accessible. Access to Experts for mentorship and mentoring should be available.

And when an employee moves out, the person moving in should be able to access the ex-employee's knowledge infrastructure to continue the operations. Experiential knowledge[33] should not get eroded. Preservation of the circles of knowledge should be independent and the Knowledge availability needs to be process-driven, rather than person-dependent.

BUSINESS LIFECYCLE AND TURNOVER

Here is a set of significant challenges that businesses face during their day-to-day operations:

- Developing a product for the market
- Expanding to a new region
- Recruiting 1000 employees in 3 months and making them productive

- Establishing customer support to increase customer satisfaction
- Increasing overall perception of the market
- To enhance productivity in the areas/needs to list practical knowledge

With 100s of projects, and pressing needs to solve and execute projects, the energy and focus of the team would be to complete the milestones, activities and match with the tastes of the customers. Such challenges may affect them critically and they may start worrying about managing knowledge. Hence, the organization needs to deliberately spend time and resources to make sure the execution happens smoothly, from Just-in-time Toyota-concept to Just-in-time knowledge is what is essential.

Knowledge has become an essential need and must be made available as an essential service.

Example: If I need to make a call and the phone is in the next room, it would be a great inconvenience. In a similar fashion, if the needed templates, know-how and context details are not handy, one spends time searching it. Let's say if there is no SOP or Body of knowledge[34], then the staff needs to spend lots of time putting the basic things in place.

The overall advantages of knowledge management systems are represented in the below table. Organizations are doing KM in various forms and labels. It is essential that a focused approach should be established in every organization to develop such knowledge infrastructures.

The importance of following the principles of ISO 30401 KMS is important, it can be used as the reference material to developing one's KM infrastructures.

Ontological Level	Challenges	KMS benefits	Standard Impact
Global	Competition	Effective Decisions	30401 Compliant Eco-System
Inter-nations	Disruptive markets-	Efficiency of processes	Common Reference KM Model for Org., Partners, Vendors, Clients Company, Customer organization, Manufacturers, Suppliers
Nations	Ex: New technology	Enhancements	
Regional/States	New biz. Model	Org. Resilience	
Knowledge Societies	Political Dynamics	Operational Efficiency	
Institutes	Geographical spread	Adaptability	
Academics	Emerging Economical landscape	Competitive Advantage	
Cross-Industry	Dynamics of Employee association with organization	Creation, practices, apply, reuse	
Segment-based	Work from Home	Sharing practices, expertise, learning across the org boundaries	Better value chain of KM done in a specific way
Organizations	Knowledge silos	Collaboration between organization	Common understanding emerges in terms of Learning
Corporates	Knowledge Erosions	Highly visible knowledge	Explicit KM Practitioners reference
Startups	Scattered information	Eco-system for sharing	Org Impetus for KM as Critical Function
NGO's	Experts bandwidth challenges	Frees experts bandwidth	Org. of every Size to Embrace KM
Bottom of the Pyramid	Geographically dispersed teams	Connected with high collaboration	Focused Knowledge Retention
Professional Discipline	Stop Gap employment	Delivery Excellence	Easier KM Buy-in at C-Suite
Role based	Professional Growth very slow	Steer towards Learning organizations	Possibility of KM Unicorns
Context-based	Unclear Career paths	Foundation to every Initiative	Compliments Innovation Standard
Time/Space/nature-based	Significantly Low KM Job Market	Greater demand for KM professionals	

Diagram: K.M.S.A 1 – KM Standard Advantages – few listed

Whether the organization wishes to go for certification or not, that is irrelevant. The important question is by applying these KM principles, has the organization been able to focus on solving knowledge problems holistically?

Has the organization been able to enhance collaboration and knowledge-sharing experience among employees, clients, customers, partners, contractors, vendors, etc.?

Has the organization established a working culture where sharing happens naturally, where innovations and knowledge management is proactively addressed in every activity being done?

As an organization, how are we addressing knowledge silos, knowledge erosion due to employee turnover?

How can organizations increase productivity and efficiency by sharing best practices, case studies, methodologies, a body of knowledge within and reducing the invention of the wheel every time they face a similar situation, problem, etc.?

Especially during and the post-pandemic world, where work from home option could become the new norm of working, how has the organization reinvented itself to provide the required knowledge infrastructure to enhance collaboration, decrease isolations and share knowledge among one and all?

Has the organization used knowledge management philosophy[35] in developing KM strategy in every aspect of organization functions, projects, service lines, customer management, technology management, etc.?

The possibilities to create results by applying the KM Philosophies are infinite. The best part of KM is it can be applied to any role you are currently playing, you can make a difference to your teams, organization units or business units, projects, organizations, companies with a focused KM approach and by designing KM systems. We will discover what are these KM systems. Is it a technology? Do I need to spend a lot of money? Do I need to invest in expensive software? These are some of the first thoughts which surface in the mind of those who are not familiar with KM.

Knowledge management is applicable universally to any company, organization regardless of industry or segment.

Knowledge Management is about nurturing people's potential by developing the learning and sharing culture.

The most effective Knowledge management tool is Conversations.

The most effective Knowledge Management practice is to Look, Practice and Learn.

The most important people who are needed for KM are from every Role in the organization.

The most effective knowledge capture technique is Questioning.

The critical requirement for KM workability is Trust.

The primary outcomes of good Knowledge Management are Innovations, Efficiency and Productivity!

Knowledge Management is not an option, but a critical function in every organization.

CHAPTER FOUR

KMS SCOPE - BREADTH AND WIDTH

MAPPING THE ORGANIZATIONAL LANDSCAPE

Knowledge management requirements vary from one team to another, from one function to another, from one organization to another with such a diverse landscape of knowledge management. It is essential to determine the scope of the KMS designed for the organization.

Every organization's knowledge needs are different, hence the context of the organization needs to be understood first.

Here, the primary intention is to determine the scope of the knowledge management system based on the organization's decomposition/functional decomposition analysis along with identifying the critical business, interested parties, determining their knowledge challenges and then converting them from a business domain into the knowledge domain.

Organizational Level (Example)	Functional Areas
	Department Areas
	Value Streams areas
	Inter department areas
	Intra department areas
Project Level (example)	Reusable Knowledge Units
	Experts network and mentorship
	Onboarding and learning management
	Experiential learning
	Competency and skills development
	Management, Technical, Non-technical skills enhancement
	Collaboration, knowledge sharing and exchange culture embeddedness

Diagram K.M.L 1 – KM Layers example

LIFECYCLES

KMS depends on various life cycles of domains, topics, subjects, roles, fields, discipline, organizational functions, department, service line, business unit, sales marketing, etc. This should be considered from the knowledge entity's life-cycle perspective. And once you are aware of which life-cycle you have chosen during the scoping work, you would also look at what knowledge layers you are focusing on – additional dimension.

KNOWLEDGE LAYERS

KMS lifecycle can occur, converge, diverge, form, reshape, convolute in these knowledge layer's dimension. There are physical spaces, digital spaces[36], social spaces[37] and time zones. Times zones/Time in itself in the sense, past, present, future. When we talk about physical spaces, we are referring to the office, service center, sales showroom, the real estate offices or, where people interact together, where they sit together, work together, manufacturing units, sales units, drilling assets, etc. The physicalness of the office is the physical space.

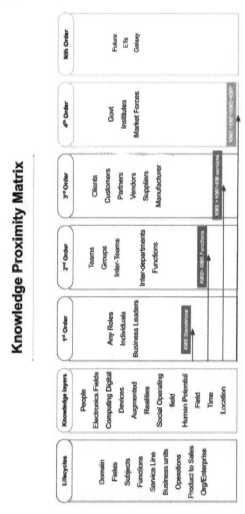

Diagram K.P.M 1- Knowledge Proximity Matrix

The other dimension we have to look at is the digital spaces. Again, as an individual, I have my e-mail, I have my shared boxes. I have my dairy, drive, etc. These are my first individual digital spaces. Then, there is our team's digital space. Then, the inter-department digital space. Then the external digital space. These are other dimensions as well that we have to look at. How do you look at this digital space? How do you manage the content in this digital space? What knowledge do you need, what is available, etc. are some of the elements in this digital space.

The other space, which we must look at is the social spaces, where we look at the people in terms of teams, departments, intra-organization, inter-organization, external to the organization, internal to the organization, clients, customers, where there's interaction, conversation, dialogue, etc. All these add to the knowledge layers that must be considered. It involves talking to people and finding people outside the organization for the knowledge needed today and in the future, considering every dimension of knowledge management and its life-cycle.

KNOWLEDGE NEED- ORDER

The Knowledge Proximity[38] Orders are the distance from one's knowledge needs to the difficulties which need to be addressed to smoothen the knowledge flow. The higher the order of knowledge proximity, the greater is the challenge to share. See the Diagram K.P.M 1- Knowledge Proximity Matrix Model.

So firstly, we need to understand the knowledge management system which in itself has a broad spectrum of assembling of the first order, second order, third order, fourth order, nth order knowledge needs. Therefore, we need to develop a knowledge management system based on the proximity of knowledge needs.

First Order- Knowledge Needs are the perspective of Self, the immediate roles, the role of knowledge creators. What is my role? What immediate knowledge do I need? Do I have access to it? Every knowledge I need should be within my close proximity or my reach as I think it should be available.

As the knowledge Sources move to a different order, the challenges and complexity to access knowledge from the perspective of self become more demanding and distanced.

KMS foundations should be based on either of these two elemental foundations and one or more Knowledge Proximity Orders to develop a holistic approach.

STANDALONE KM AND KM FUNCTION

There are multiple constructs of knowledge management systems in existence or could come into existence at organizations.

a. Standalone KMS

This KMS is standalone in nature, which means that the knowledge management system in itself is not Management or top-down driven. There are no KM functions[39] institutionalized by corporate. It could be driven by an individual role in a team or it could be developed by the manager role. There could be various functions driving KM principles using various labels and names. These are embedded within the various department functional activities and various systems are developed by these functions and departments.

Majority of the readers would agree that most of you would be having some kind of standalone knowledge management systems, which might be with a different label and these are all standalone systems working as part of the IT department or working to facilitate the workshop, train and mentor people, etc.

b. KM Function

Now moving up the ladder in terms of deployment of knowledge management systems, is looking at having a knowledge management function and developing knowledge management services from the requirement of the organization. And over a period of time, knowledge management practices should be developed, which are a set of framework tools, templates, guides, how to set procedures. These should be designed in a way that these could be reused and implemented and easily accessible to anybody in the organization, first to follow and create an outcome of certain management practice.

INTERESTED PARTIES AND KM SCOPING

We have two important inputs taken from the organization decomposition and the knowledge business challenges in terms of Knowledge proximity order.

Based on knowledge proximity, you could choose the stakeholders, in turn, they would help in identifying their key business challenges. Also, it is important to understand, while defining the scope, whichever function or the value stream has the largest population dwelling into a common knowledge pool, that could also be an important criterion.

If you are using the Pareto formula, it is always better to look at 80% of the knowledge utilized by the 20% KM system. So you need to streamline knowledge needs for maximum impact in those areas.

Now let me reiterate the business challenges through an example:

1. The first order is considering two to three significant challenges related to the customer contact center. One possibility could be that critically most of the agents are putting the calls on long haul time to find information. Another could be, one is seeking knowledge for one's own consumption.

2. The second-order is the marketing team trying to call various accounts to find out their reports and understand customer feedback. Similarly, the second-order need is also from the sales team to get all the presentation brochures. And it could be taking a lot of time for them to find the right information at the right time, this is one of the major challenges. Knowledge sources are dependent on people from different teams or groups.

3. The third order and requirement perspective are the management is not able to get hands-on on some of the important market related comparative information. The knowledge is neither available directly nor with any person; it needs to be sourced with commercial charges.

Scoping Example:

30 Customer care representatives catering to 1 million customers; this means the knowledge flow and knowledge

availability for these agents need to be streamlined and should be one of the areas covered under KMS Scope-Customer Service Lifecycle.

If Project delivery is the primary execution unit in the organization, managing its knowledge would be very effective. The scope could be at Project Delivery Lifecycle.

So, the scope could be to solve the First Order Knowledge needs or Second-Order Knowledge needs.

Trying to solve the Third Order Knowledge needs gets more challenging, and the focus could be more on classical KM[40] for the collaboration, conversation and engagements to produce effective results.

There are various competitive advantage business areas, which need improvement or require focus and need knowledge development.

So it is important, once you identify these criteria, you also need to identify the reasons why the challenges are occurring currently. What are these reasons, why these challenges started are cropping up? What are the data points and what are the historical implications because of these challenges? What are the reasons which have led to this business problem?

And it is very important to have all these data points documented in your knowledge management business case document.

In the next chapter, we will unravel that the organization has multiple focus areas like operational function, marketing/sales function, R&D (Research and Development) function, etc., but we will limit our scope to marketing and sales function to discuss and design a KMS at a generic level as an example. It will provide a practical step-by-step approach in designing a knowledge management system in a given context, aligned to ISO 30401 Standard.

CHAPTER FIVE

KMS

Every organization should develop its own KM System framework[41] that is aligned with the ISO 30401 requirements. In the diagram K.M.S.D 1, the KMS framework has been mapped to the standard requirement clauses to provide a general understanding of how to align one's KM program. This also provides you an overall understanding of the Knowledge Management System Framework implementation toolkit to illustrate how one can develop one's custom framework for an easy understanding of the KM function and the organizational knowledge workers[42]. Detailed steps and approach have been shared for the first two phases as an example.

In this chapter, we are going to learn about the knowledge management system in general. The knowledge management system has multiple dimensions that need to be established, implemented, maintained and with continuous improvement.

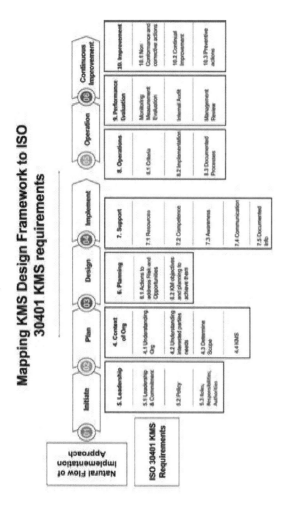

Diagram K.M.S.D 1 – Knowledge Management System Design Framework

KMS LIFECYCLE AND FRAMEWORK

The KMS Development Lifecycle has multiple phases to make KMS effective and add value to businesses. They are as follows:

1. Initiate
2. Plan
3. Design
4. Implement
5. Operation
6. Continuous Improvement

1. **Initiate**: In the initiation phase, the leadership initiates the KM program or project[43] for an organization, providing the required leadership and sponsorship. The leadership brings together a team to work on the KM project and develop a comprehensive KM policy for the organization.

2. **Plan**: The KM team starts to develop a business case with a detailed organizational context, developing mapping of the interested parties, identifying the key business challenges to solve in the knowledge domain by scoping. The team develops the KMS solutions for the organization to solve the business challenges.

Phase Procedure steps:

- Develop Organization/Functional Decomposition[44] mapping
- Identify Key stakeholders/Interested Parties
- Develop Knowledge Proximity Order Matrix – for the interested parties by engaging them in workshops
- Develop detailed 8 folds KM Planning
- Develop a RACI matrix[45] for the organization

Phase input:

- Organization's Decomposition Mapping Documents
- Functional Decomposition Mapping Documents

- Knowledge Proximity Order Matrix Document
- Minutes
- Survey Forms
- Interview Transcript

Phase Outputs:

- Business Case for KM program/initiative
- Business KM requirements documents[46]
- KM Architecture Planning Document[47]
- KM Blueprint Documents
- Team Workspaces
- Document Sharing workspace[48]
- Forums to discuss[49]

Guides/SOP

- Organization Decomposition Procedures
- Functional Decomposition Procedure
- KM Self-Assessment Report[50]
- KM Roadmap Document[51]
- KM Proximity Order Matrix Procedure

Template

- Organization Decomposition Template
- Functional Decomposition Template
- Action Tracker Template
- KM Architecture Planning Template
- RACI Matrix Templates
- Minutes of Meetings Template

3. **Design**:

Based on KM Blueprint and roadmap, start designing the KM solution[52]. This is the most critical phase of the KM lifecycle which is based on the assessments at the enterprise level or knowledge entity level design KM initiatives. Refer to Diagram K.I.F 1 – KMS Implementation Framework[53]. There are few fundamental knowledge blocks that are critical or foundational KM blocks which are necessary regardless of the type of industry, segment, or size of the organization.

- Establish the role of KM SPOCS for KM systems/ Initiatives in every function or knowledge entities

Foundation Block 1: Establish Knowledge asset management[54] program

- Conduct Knowledge Asset management (KAM) Workshop/engagement sessions
- The KAM workshop may span over multiple working sessions
- KAM could be at the Macro or Micro-level
- In the workshops/engagement sessions
  - Determine the Approach needed
  - Determine the Organizational area
  - Determine the KAM solution
  - Design KAM solution
  - Design KAM system
  - Design KPI
  - Design Evangelization Plan
  - Plan for Operationalization and Support

Foundation Block 2: Establish Onboarding and Learning Management[55]

- Determine Competency and Skills requirement
- Design Onboarding Systems to reduce the learning curve
- Establish Subject and Topic-Based Forums
- Design Macro and Micro Onboarding System
- Establish Internal and External Collaboration
- Establish Local, Regional and International Collaboration
- Plan for Operationalization and Support

Foundation Block 3: Establish Lesson-Learned Knowledge system[56]

- Conduct LL Workshop to gather requirements
- Establish the Change Management Process
- Design the LL system, LL process and LL Deployment Plan
- Develop KPI Systems
- Facilitate Peer-to-Peer Sharing Workshops
- Plan for Operationalization and Support

Foundation Block 4: Establish Experts and Collaboration Systems[57]

- Map Expertise
- Develop Expertise Map
- Develop Community of Practices (CoPs)
- Mature CoPs

- Plan for Operationalization and Support
- Guidelines (Define Foundational blocks as per the organizational needs)

Phase Inputs

- Templates Filled by interested parties
- Conversations Feedback
- Forums Feedback
- Surveys Outcomes
- Meetings Outcomes

Phase Outputs

- Foundational KM System Solution Design
- Developing Knowledge Asset Management System Procedures
- Developing Onboarding and Learning Management System Procedures
- Lesson Learned Knowledge System Implementation Procedure
- Developing Expert systems and CoP's Implementation Procedures
- Moderators and Users Guides
- Knowledge Exchange Facilitation[58]
- Lesson Workshop Facilitation Guidelines
- Innovation and Knowledge Strategy Facilitation Guidelines
- Highly Effective Knowledge Sharing Workshops
- Enhanced Collaboration with Interested Parties

- Taxonomy Mapping
- Knowledge Asset Mapping
- Process Asset Mapping
- Work-Activities-Tasks Mapping
- Process Documentation Mapping
    - Technical Documentation
    - Skills and Development Roadmap
    - Resources and Mentor Mapping
    - Lesson Capture Process Development
    - Lessons Reuse Process Declaration
    - Organizational Learning Embedding Tracker
    - Experts Profiling Template
    - Themes Setup Questionnaire
    - Peer to Peer Sharing Templates
    - Lessons Review Templates
    - Innovation and Knowledge Management Development Working Sheets
    - Taxonomy Development Working Sheet

4. **Implement**

5. **Operation**

6. **Continuous Improvement**

The 4, 5 and 6 phases are covered in detail in the upcoming chapters. In the next section, we will see how a KM solution takes shape during the implementation phase.

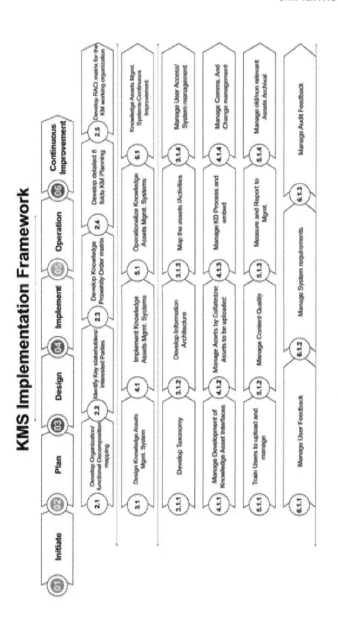

Diagram K.I.F 1 – KMS Implementation Framework

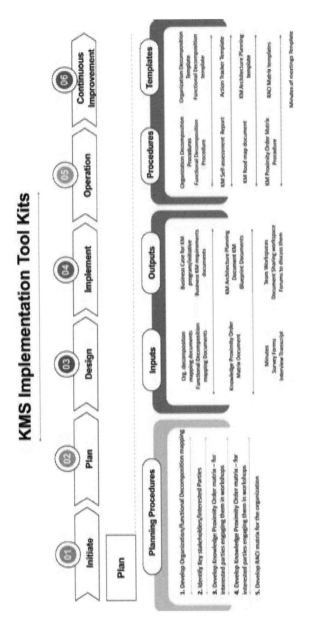

Diagram K.I.F.P 2- KMS Implementation Framework Plan

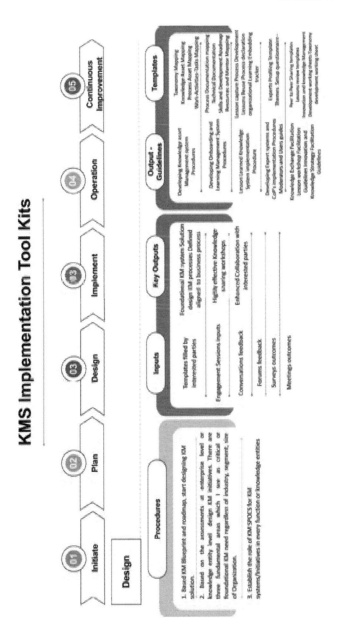

Diagram K.I.F.D 3- KMS Implementation Framework Design

MARKETING AND SALES FUNCTIONAL KM DESIGN

As this book cannot cover the entire KM solution platter; it would become voluminous to include in one book, so we will cover the salient area and use the 10 steps guide to roll out KM solutions.

10 STEPS GUIDE TO ROLL OUT KM SOLUTIONS

1. Develop Business Case for the Function
2. Capture the Knowledge Landscape of the Function
3. Developing Marketing Circle of Knowledge based on Sales and Marketing Roles
4. Mapping Taxonomy involving – Assets, Artifacts Type, Experts, Geographical Locations, Working Units, etc.
5. Proposing KM Solutions, Choosing 1 or 2 areas to prototype
6. Engage with Multiple Stakeholders during the design phase
7. Develop KM Solutions – Systems, Processes, Practices, Procedures, KPIs, Governance, etc.
8. Operationalize KM Systems, Manage Content and Relevancy, User Rights, Value Creation out of the system
9. Review the Value out of these initiatives, report to management
10. Continuous Improvement of the KM system based on User requirements

Ideally, what is the vision of the marketing team? We are looking at making the Knowledge Management or knowledge of the available product and updates clear and concise, make the product artifacts and other knowledge assets easily accessible and searchable. We also want to make communication seamless and have appropriate onboarding processes in place.

So, if this is our business case, for example, at this point in time, the team desires the possible outcome out of the KM Engagement.

Now, how do we go about developing a knowledge management system for this? The scope requirements and intended business user expectations have been captured. Before we start developing a knowledge management system, we need to take a couple of steps to design these systems, processes, business rules, procedures, etc.

During the planning phase, engagement with the right stakeholders is critical. It is important to map the right stakeholders who are involved in the complete marketing function. Therefore, considering the functions within the marketing and sales department, identify the key people who are going to be part of this process. Then ensure that the entire process is communicated to them. This is one of the important keys to the success of the knowledge management systems for the marketing team.

The first things you have to start after the initial kick-off meetings are to analyze:

1. What is the existing knowledge infrastructure?
2. What are the processes that are defined to capture, share, store knowledge?
3. What are the key processes leading to knowledge?
4. How do you document the changes?

5. Who are the experts in this field of marketing/sales team?

6. Where do the team members find their documents?

7. Where do the team members find artifacts?

8. Where do they find the external links and the customer contacts, et cetera?

9. Where do the product teams communicate?

10. How do they communicate?

11. What are the various internal, external communications and where are they stored?

12. In what format are they stored, etc.?

13. How do you find the competitive intelligence (CI)[59] of the competitors?

14. What mechanism or process or system is available to provide the CI?

So these are some examples of the important questions to be asked. Once these questions have been answered, there are other couple of questions which are more related to:

1. How do you train the new member or how do you onboard a new member?

2. What are the methods and practices at present?

3. How do you manage and learn from customer interactions?

4. Also, are we going to look at what are the various digital spaces?

5. What are the physical spaces?

6. Which are the portals the team uses?

7. Where and how do they collect the materials for the onboarding?

8. What is the training for the people, to people, is digital training in place?

9. Are the lessons captured on an on-going basis?

10. How is the sharing happening within the team, etc.?

This questionnaire provides an in-depth analysis of the existing knowledge management landscape, the challenges, and the gaps which are a part of the design phase. So these gaps are going to provide us an impetus to design the knowledge management solutions.

While circulating this questionnaire, the factors that need to be considered are if it's a large group or small group, can it be done through a one-on-one interview or focused group workshops or capturing information through surveys and questionnaires.

Conducting a brainstorming session[60] would also yield great knowledge challenge points and an existing knowledge landscape. i.e. get the flare of the overall explicit and tacit knowledge spread[61]. This information would support in the development of the KM solutions. The other methods could be walking the floor, observing employees; their environment and their tasks could provide a great number of data points too.

Overall, once you have a sense of the team functioning, you can identify knowledge management or mismanagement, knowledge landscape and the people's expertise; how the team learning happens, how onboarding happens, how knowledge is retained, how the experts, mentors juniors, etc. share knowledge.

Based on the above assessment, you would be familiar to suggest solutions for critical business areas. There could be one or two areas where the KM solution can be taken up as a pilot for practical illustration and get buy-in from users within the department.

So these are the questions that would give us inputs to develop the KM blueprint for Marketing. Based on the knowledge of the challenges at hand, a few recommendations for the marketing team are as follows:

1. Develop a centralized knowledge management system for all the knowledge assets

2. A need for a centralized dashboard for communication

3. Centralized expert profiles should be available for the team to make sure all the expertise and experiences are available

4. Learning and competency management system to onboard trainees/laterals

5. And there is also a requirement to develop the body of knowledge on how to go about doing things, how to handle, develop various case studies and success stories, stories to be added as part of learnings for the newbies

These are some of the KM streams which need to be addressed for the marketing and sales team, however, Proposal 1 and 4 will be taken up as prototyping in this book to illustrate the practical steps.

So, one of the important activities is to develop the taxonomy[62], which captures the essence of the entire activities of marketing/sales, entire assets which are used, presentation name, et cetera.

Does it help in identifying the different phases, processes of team management, overall design, etc.? All these inputs can be of significant help during the design phase.

Now, we have a process, a high level of the process which captures every step of the entire knowledge management design phase, which not only includes the design phase but an overall knowledge management system and the steps on how you can design here.

When you start initiating the kick-off with the support of the leadership team, you are going to map, as I mentioned, assess various areas of:

- knowledge assets,
- experts,
- how-tos,
- key critical knowledge[63] and
- see how you can design the knowledge management solution, like
    - building knowledge management as an asset repository,
    - to build an expert's people directory,
    - to design a question and answer,
    - a Quora kind of community,
    - And what are the existing technologies which are there in the hand?

Engaging stakeholders is a must in each of these processes. Therefore, conducting workshops to find out their requirements, their aspirations, and their challenges is a must.

As you do it, communication is also important before the meetings and after the workshops. Action and agreed requirements need to be captured. Apart from capturing the action, it has to be made available, communicated and agreed upon within the stakeholders of that particular workshop and the charter. Once this charter agrees, this has to be submitted and agreed upon with the review team, also the management of the team.

Once it is named, then the sign off can be done to implement the solution. So the solution has multiple levels.

Thus, during the design phase, all this required information is captured and forwarded to the development team or the technology team or the knowledge management team to design a system, design a repository and may make the knowledge management system portal go live.

If you have to develop a technology from the scratch, it is going to take 12 to 18 months for the entire technology, commercial and vendor selection, RFP (Request for Proposal) evaluation, finalizing the commercials and having the infrastructure like servers and other things built/ procured for an organization. And then the customization and development process would start eventually. So, that is one way of looking at the technology infrastructure.

If the technology infrastructure is already in place, then this whole process becomes much easier. If you are customizing and developing custom solutions, again, this may take lesser time, but still, it cut-shorts the commercialization, vendor selection and other phases of developing the infrastructure, assuming the technology is in place. So, these are some of the infrastructure cycles that an organization needs to go through as a part of the implementation phase.

Developing highly visible knowledge portals, what is essential is the accessibility with ease; any information which you can access within 2 clicks can be called "Just-in-Time Knowledge Visibility[64]". The importance of content is what makes it clear and uncluttered based on the taskonomy. Before we proceed, let me share; this book doesn't have the scope to dwell into Digital Knowledge Management[65].

Below are some illustrations that show how the knowledge repositories need to be designed. These illustrations help in understating how one accesses the knowledge, the purpose behind accessing the document, application of the artifacts, etc. This book will not cover the KM-IT system implementation phase.

KEY KNOWLEDGE ATTRIBUTES

Diagram – K.A.T.A.T 1 – Knowledge Asset Taxonomy Attribute Type- Example

The above image provides a glimpse of mapping all the knowledge assets of the marketing/sales department (refer to Appendix-V for detailed taxonomy for Marketing and Sales Function). Each node represents the explicit Knowledge of the team required for daily operation and management of the Marketing & Sales Function.

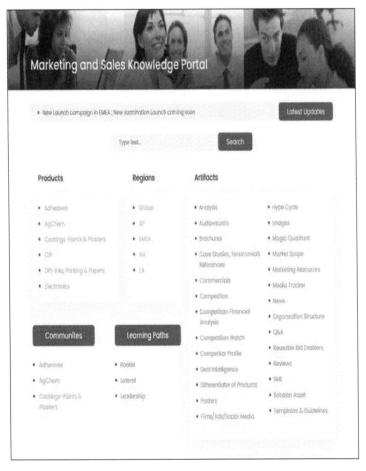

Diagram H.V.K.R 1-Highly Visible Knowledge Repositories - Example

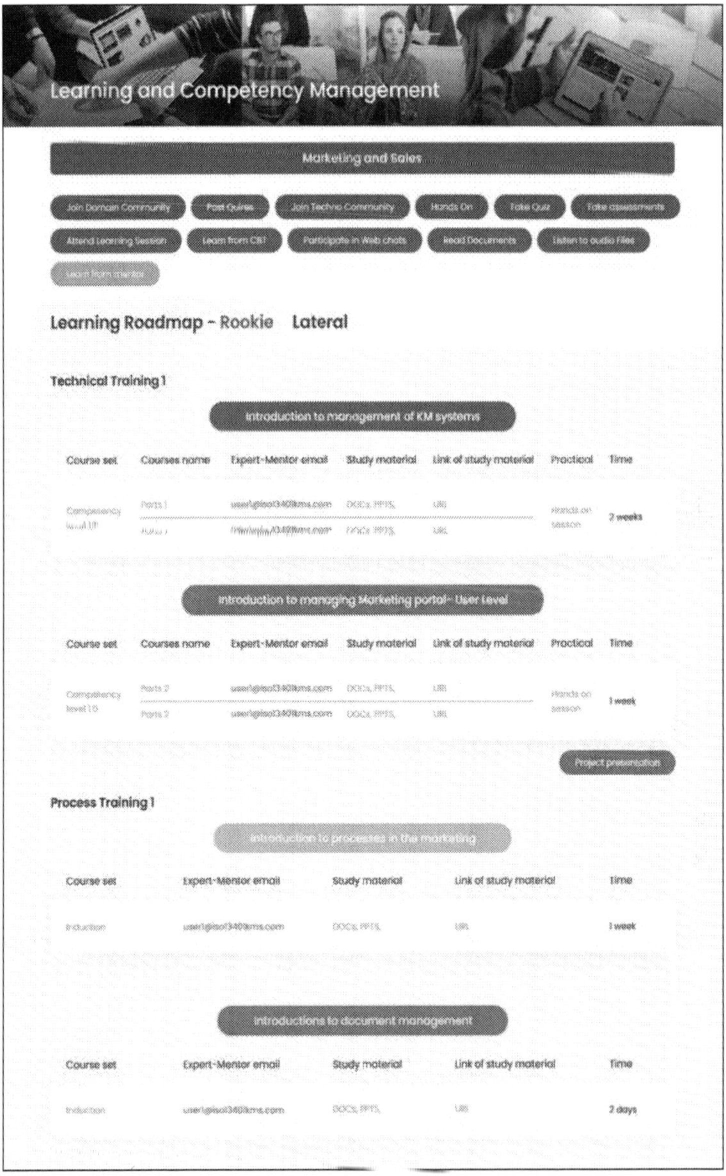

Diagram L.C.M 1- Learning and Competency Management System - Example

Once the systems are ready to go live, integrate the portal task and activity with the business process, the proper experts are mapped. During the implementation phase, once these systems are ready, the training material has to be created, user documentation has to be created, and you also define a generic knowledge KPI in terms of engaging the audience. The contribution expected from the audience needs to be assimilated. You also look at how do you tie the various business processes into this procedure, also develop a simple change management plan and a communication plan to have this deployed across the marketing team spread across the geography.

When all these tools or the systems are about to go live or operational, you train the audience, set up meetings and engage them to test the use cases along with them. After testing, ask them to contribute and work with some of the use cases and test cases independently and provide feedback on the user usability of the system.

Then you can go with the soft launch initially. Once most of the requirements are met with the user and they are satisfied, then a big-bang communication approach can be taken up, and an e-learning module can be created, so that any user or the contributor or administration of the systems can learn through the interfaces like online or face-to-face.

So with this, you also set up the KPIs and you agree with the management on the progress, update with the progress, and have the processes developed. You get the blessings in terms of a way to integrate the process and in the philosophy, procedures. So if we gauge the progress at this point, we will find, there could be multiple challenges in terms of content management, content purging and content development. We also have to look at the expert's participation in various knowledge sharing sessions, experts mentoring various mentees. Also, encourage the experts to answer the question of the various other teams, and the leadership must also participate in this community by answering questions. This way, there's unique participation and a synergy is created within the marketing team where collaboration, coordination and communication occur simultaneously with the exchanging of assets, reusable assets, how-to cases, good stories, best practices, and it can become seamless.

The Diagram H.V.K.P 1: Example of Highly Visible Knowledge Repositories showcases how one can easily access knowledge artifacts with ease. Over a period of time, the systems could be made much more robust and user-friendly with continuous feedback on performance and usability challenges based on human ergonomics.

The Diagram L.C.M 1 provides learning and the competency management system model provides a framework to map the individual with the learning path when somebody joins the team, department as a rookie or experienced employee.

So over a period of time, capture some of these good practices and share them with the organization to showcase how a knowledge management system could add productivity, or cut down the customer conversion cycle, et cetera. These are some of the processes or some of the steps in terms of a knowledge management system that can create value for the marketing team. These are some of the typical steps involved in developing a, I would not say, perfect system, but it would at least capture 60 to 80% of the knowledge, explicit knowledge management, and have a strong 20% to 40% of tacit knowledge. Experts may be available to create that environment so that they can train the other 80% of the team, which is again an important aspect of knowledge sharing. So, this provides a sense of how a knowledge management system could be developed in a small team, which is spread across various locations. In these ways, the functional-circle of knowledge is established. Again, the content could become outdated very fast, hence devise a good strategy to archive the content based on lifecycle policy.

This is a typical life cycle of KMS, and this provides a simple and generic level of identifying the knowledge areas, assessing the existing landscape, developing the KM solution and implementing the solution. It can bolster in upgrading the knowledge management services with continuous improvement embedded into the system. This is the typical life cycle of a given system. If you are starting from scratch, it would take from 3 months to 12 months. If the technology is already in place, it might take a few weeks to a couple of months, provided all the conditions apply like provided all the inputs, stakeholder's participation, IT budgeting, IT development requirements and resources are available and agreed to be completed within a certain timeline.

Based on my own experience, this is a typical natural flow of how a knowledge management program works in various organizations.

Developing documentation based on the requirements could be easily mapped based on our natural way of doing things and then mapping it to the requirement clause, which I have illustrated in the functional diagram.

CHAPTER SIX

LEADERSHIP

Leadership steering is essential to set up a knowledge management system at the enterprise level, in business units, or service units, and other large scale knowledge entities. Leadership is also of paramount significance wherever KM is being driven as an organizational initiative that involves budgeting, resourcing, change management involving multi-parties.

In my opinion, making KMS successful is the responsibility of each knowledge worker, therefore, one must be responsible for managing one's knowledge effectively. This is a powerful statement and can create an unbelievable ecosystem to develop the natural culture of pro-sharing and innovation.

For example:

In an organization's support call center, the team had to support customers across the globe on the banking queries. The client had started a new business outside the country to tap into non-resident citizen's income. The product manual website and other information were given to the support group.

Over a period of time, the call duration increased, hence the customer hold time also increased, and some customers used to get dropped off while waiting for the support agent to respond. The management was very worried as the customers started complaining to the clients about the long wait, which made the customers hang-up. This led to high call drops that were increasing per day, because of which the customers started complaining about the bad customer service support. As a remedial step, the management tried to do multiple training and awareness sessions for the customer support team. However, it seemed impossible to address the root cause.

This got escalated as there were major performance issues reported from the client to the support center management. Meanwhile, one of the team members was frustrated with finding the scattered information and switching to various portals/file drives/open multiple documents to retrieve information regarding banking products. That member started organizing, collating all the information about the product in one single place. In one click, all the information was available easily for the support staff. This reduced the frequency and the number of times the customer agents put the customer on hold. Other staff members also started using this knowledge-base. And within a few weeks, the call drop rate and the customer hold time decreased significantly as the support staff could find all the information, different catalogs, product information available at a click. They stopped searching in multiple portals, multiple logins to find the required information. They took all the updating documents on the portal for the information in client updates.

This case story is important because of the standalone initiative by an employee within the team. **In general, the Business Manager's focus and importance are laid primarily to manage the business operation, Clients, liquidity, physical assets, customer relationship, quality, profitability,** etc. However, the Business Leaders should extend their focus on creating knowledge leaders in multiple layers of the organization as well. No human mind can see all the constraints about knowledge needs at different orders. And it's next to impossible for a few people to understand everybody's persisting knowledge challenges and develop a solution to set all the ducks in a row.

In the scheme of running an organization, it is paramount for the organization to keep an eye open for the employees who self-motivate and go the extra mile to work beyond the KPIs. The leadership should be efficient in managing the knowledge of the team projects and knowledge entities, etc. Although it's about local leadership, global leaders also need to develop such knowledge leadership on the ground and foster an innovation culture. When individuals, teams, projects, and other organizational entities start taking ownership of their knowledge needs and manage their own knowledge, the knowledge leadership from management would be very successful in building a learning organization[66].

And in turn, the organization can build trust in these leaders, work with them to develop the knowledge management infrastructure. The organization can work with the business leaders with the tool of knowledge management support to develop an organization's knowledge management blueprint. It is important for us to understand a KM in different organizational contexts and how management or leadership works.

There are several organizations with multi-dimensions. Some dimensions are related to the client-facing organization. Others could be on product-development organizations, service-oriented organizations, research, academic institutes, government institutes and so on. So there is a need for a KM committee and KM champion to steer the KM functions, so that review happens periodically and frequently to monitor the progress of the KM Program executions.

	KM Committee	KM Functions	KM Champions	Reviews
Stand-Alone KM	N/A	N/A	Yes	N/A
Client Facing Org.	Yes	Yes	Yes	Yes
Product Development Org.	Yes	Yes	Yes	Yes
Service Oriented Org.	Yes	Yes	Yes	Yes
Research/Academics	Yes	Yes	Yes	Yes
Government/Institutes	Yes	Yes	Yes	Yes

Diagram K.M.E.F.S 1- KM Entities Functional Structure examples

The following steps are important to steer KM Programs in the organizations or knowledge entities:

- Analyze the knowledge flow between external and internal KM requirements.
- Assign a KM program for every client to manage knowledge.

- Direct KM function to develop KM solutions that are aligned with the overall business strategy.

- Set up yearly, quarterly and monthly meetings with KM function and business leader to report the progress made on knowledge management.

- The KM team/Function should set up meetings with the business leaders and report the KM program, engagement, effectiveness, and collaboration metrics to the business leaders.

- As KM functions develop KM portfolios on similar clients and manage KM, so these should be introduced and projected to either the management or the client.

- Work with the core team in each client to establish the design, implement and support the KM system.

- Within the KM function, have a status review to understand these good practices on the overall KM portfolio, KM project status and every account or the client KM outcomes.

- Derive the value from systems and data points to prepare KM reports monthly.

- In this report, each of the document assets, reusable documents submitted, learnings submitted and contributor's metrics should be measured.

- At the same time, the number of users accessing, downloading, their declaration of outcome and effective usage to be documented in that report.

- KM function should hold a meeting with the business leadership quarterly and yearly to discuss the future business challenge and develop a KM strategy[67] aligning with them.

- The reporting structure needs to be established by leadership in this way. The key is the reporting structure drivers by considering top to bottom, across the horizon and depths of the organization. Instead of providing the ground reality, it's good to have some numbers.

The recommendation related to leadership accountability structure, in many ways, is an example in large organization client-based software development, engineering and other allied services. Similarly, leaders should create an accountability matrix for KM portfolio, incentive programs and projects in an institutional way. These are also important elements of governance.

KNOWLEDGE MANAGEMENT POLICY

Knowledge Management Policy is the heart of KM function in an organization. In the last case we discussed that procedures and manuals, SOPs (Standard Operating Procedures) were developed and were integrated with the business process and employee's yearly KPIs (Key Performance Indicators) for the marketing and sales function.

These are generally guided by KM policies.

If the organization has a KM function or any function whose role is to manage the organizational knowledge, then it is important for the management to stress on developing a knowledge management policy for the organization.

This is very important as it will show the true intent to its employees about the knowledge management and leadership commitment for the same. If the organization is going for the ISO 30401 certificate or wants to declare itself as an ISO

30401 KMS requirement compliant, this document is one of the prime requirements.

The policy should provide a generic framework and guiding principles. For example:

- The policies should state the purpose of why is the KM necessary.
- What is the vision?
- What is the mission of the organization and how KM is aligned to fulfill the business outcomes? They should provide a high level for a framework in terms of the strategic framework on KM.

The policy should specifically highlight for example:

- What is your KM vision?
- What is your policy on KM performance management?
- What is your KM storage policy?
- What is your KM review on the archival policy?
- What is your knowledge creation policy?
- What is your knowledge management policy?
- What are your controls and knowledge that are a part of the policy?
- What is your KM backup policy?
- What is the KM access control policy?
- What is your policy on KM communications?
- What are your storage and guidelines policies?
- What are your change management guidelines?
- What are your good practices and learning guidelines?

- What are your technology and definitions for the KM (Glossaries)?
- What are the KM access control procedures?
- What are your communication procedures?
- What is your KM orientation program?
- What is your change management procedure?
- What are knowledge management, knowledge creation procedures?
- What are the KM review procedures?
- What are the story procedures and what are the backup policies?

It is important to have the policies drafted and the same must be communicated to the employees across the organization. The policies must be communicated in a way that they are understood and followed by employees.

ROLES, RESPONSIBILITY AND AUTHORITIES

In the last case, it was important to define roles and activities:

- When to report, what is the frequency of reporting?
- How is the performance measured?
- What criteria are defined as KM measurement, etc.?

In my experience, the KM is the last priority when it comes to completing schedules or launching products or completing services for organizational employees.

The project manager is under constant pressure to have the projects completed within the budget. Each of the leadership roles is under constant pressure, because of things happening, at the same time, also because of the things not happening, which were supposed to happen. So every day, there's firefighting to move things, to make things happen. Management pressures and reporting status; red, amber, yellow keep, the managers on toes. This kind of premise is set for the leadership team to work with the knowledge worker or the central function. The project managers are constantly strained by who needs to deliver the milestone and get the quality right.

The key is to interact and complete work, jobs and activities. If somebody undergoes this situation from morning till night, and this happens every day, then probably the trigger of 'sell our product' gets activated. In such a situation, where is the time for knowledge management? So practically speaking, having the KM system, having KM function, having leadership support are only half battle won in KM.

The full battle is won only when the KM engagement happens with employees and the core knowledge management principles are embedded in everyday actions to enhance productivity and effectiveness. If KM can empower the knowledge experience of a project manager, it indeed has value added to the leader. In turn, he would become more supportive towards the KM.

Some of the key questions that may surface are:

- How do we overcome this challenge?
- What methods are required?
- How to drive KM effectiveness at the end of the day?
- How do you make KM relevant to leadership, middle management and managers?

From the lens of my experience, there are several ways of addressing it. There are various KM systems and processes which can be implemented that can develop the sharing culture without burdening the knowledge workers:

- Even if you have KMS in place, make the KMS design or user interface very simple with streamlined input and output designs and easier methods for submission or sharing method.

- Streamlining the entire process from creation to modification, to sharing, to reuse as easily as possible.

- The definition of roles with respect to usage, contribution, management, reuse, facilitation, representation needs to be defined and should be communicated in a way that provides added value to the work activities of the employees and they see the value addition being created.

Now, we will look at the RACI (Responsible, Accountable, Consulted, and Informed) matrix with roles, responsibilities and who needs to be informed, who is responsible for this activity, or who is accountable for these particular activities or tasks or the processes. It could be at the project-level, program-level, enterprise-level or service-levels.

We also need to develop various accountability and responsibility matrix in terms of:

- Knowledge Management SPOCs (Single Point of Contact) RACI,

- Knowledge Management accountability and responsible matrix's,

- Knowledge Management champion RACI,

- KM functional RACI,
- KM department SOP (Standard Operating Procedure), and
- SPOCs RACI should be defined.

The whole idea here is to ensure the smooth application of local content management or knowledge management. We need to have people who are responsible and accountable for managing and sharing or using the lessons or the content or the knowledge in terms of the document.

Taking responsibility of knowledge management is crucial for every knowledge worker, whether it's the head of business, business leaders, client engagement, C-suite level or whether the middle-level manager like project managers, program manager, leads, marketing, sales or development managers, software manager, etc. The requirements of knowledge are different from middle management to C-suite level or executive level knowledge needs.

These actions at the executive and middle management levels would create a major impact on various business domains they are working under.

- They can talk about simpler KM aspect to share lessons between team members:
  - Rewards & Recognition; who does it,
  - Make sure knowledge assets are managed well,
  - Make sure knowledge assets needed by the department are shared and
  - Make available proactively, make contributions to the enterprise knowledge repositories.

- They can cultivate habits and culture to develop:
  - Case studies,
  - Working frameworks,
  - Body of knowledge related to their work areas, services, technology, practices and
  - Intellectual capital in terms of
    - Patents,
    - Trademarks,
    - Copyrights, etc.
- They can energize teams, projects and other members to share ideas in process technology and improvements.
- They can manage ideas to support improvement in business process execution activities, standards and procedures.
- They can share ideas with other relevant departments, share ideas with the management for consideration.
- They can encourage team members for continuous learning, competencies and skills development.
- They can set learning paths for new joinees.
- They can create a path for development based on new life skills and competency.
- They can encourage mentors and mentor culture.
- Respect and reward the experts or mentors who are training young or rookie employees.
- Develop a long-term coaching program for young employees, develop a local succession plan to make sure the continuity of business or the project, treat

and respect and take feedback from experts to mold the newbies, rookies or new joinees in the team.

The middle management's role in KM culture is the key to the penetration of knowledge management culture and they are the real change engines in the organization. This KM role and activities pertaining to the middle-level management needs to be defined. These can be defined when the C-suite business leader and management take accountability to strengthen the human capital, both tangible and intangible.

The management roles and responsibility, at large, need to be defined at the corporate level in the KM policy and also at the KRAs (Key Responsible Areas) or the KPI (Key Performance Indicators) at the individual performance level.

- Management needs to encourage top-performing middle-level management employees.
  - They have to enable a mechanism in HR to reward and promote individuals with an extraordinary passion for knowledge management who have gone an extra mile to cultivate knowledge sharing culture, knowledge effective capture and dissemination culture. Disciplined leaders are the ones who groom the subordinates and contribute to their development, making the team strong with good competencies.
- Management needs to understand the role.
  - KM is not somebody coming from out and doing it for the organization. It is the responsibility of the organization and management to establish accountability and responsibility and run across the organization hierarchies.

- They should understand that the organizational hierarchies are for following and sharing communication lines and does not represent knowledge flow lines.

- The management, if budget allows, should allow KM function to be established, KM technology to be established.

- Analyze if the management, startup, small firm or medium-size firm can still implement KM with some of the initiatives in terms of standalone KM system, utilize Cloud-based - IT KM system (Cloud-based Collaborative systems, Cloud-based Document management systems, etc.), utilize quality teams, inculcate the KM principles in every activity, that would help to start the knowledge management journey; it is important to have one.

- They can start conducting more physical/virtual knowledge *cafés*[68], lessons learned workshops, Gemba Walks[69], knowledge sharing sessions[70], mentor-mentee engagements, which they would be doing in different levels/labels. Looking from the knowledge management's lens would provide a much deeper and impactful perspective.

- There are hundreds of different methods of Classical and IT-based methods of KM practices[71]. It is significant how the company drafts this tactical part of KM and shares it with the employees.

- This way, collaboration, accountability could be spread across the organization, this would be based on the project or the value stream life cycle in the organization.

- It is also a fallacy to tie all the responsibilities to the leadership. It doesn't work in the knowledge domain. For this, leadership should develop roles and responsibilities apart from business roles, few knowledge roles, which focus across the horizons and verticals of the organization, develop models, frameworks from the ground, create spaces or platform to showcase Good Practices Framework with initiatives.

- The moment middle and C-suite understand this aspect to create leaders at every level, then the official roles will work effectively. **KM is everybody's job and anybody can do KM.**

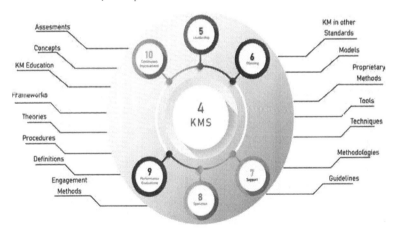

The Radial represents the KMS standard tenants with 4, 5, 6, 7, 8, 9, 10 Main clauses of requirements, based on which tools, frameworks, toolkits, software, services, methodologies, methods, etc. can be aligned or developed to cater to the needs of organization and individuals, which in itself would create the entire eco-system.

Central Clause 4 is the KMS, i.e. is the heart of the standard, which talks about ontological requirements but not a specific solution. The solutions and KM systems still need to be developed by the practitioners and organizational executives.

In fact, every C-Suite executive should have this standard as one of the important initiatives to be rolled out in the organizations.

CHAPTER SEVEN
PLANNING

Knowledge management planning is one of the most important phases in the journey of knowledge management. There are important aspects of planning, which are multifold.

We have to look from the lens of:

1. Strategic level planning,
2. Tactical level planning,
3. Operational level planning,
4. Governance level planning.
5. People engagement and change management planning,
6. Communication planning,
7. KM technology planning, and
8. KM practices planning.

Even though, the first four planning levels are the primary category of planning. However, it is important that the five to eight levels of planning are also seen independently for effective KMS strategies.

At the organization level, planning is very much critical and should cover the following layers strategic, tactical, governance, technology, KM practices. At the smaller knowledge entity level, the planning should happen at the operational level, people engagement communication level. The planning phase is again what connects to the organizational context and the scope of knowledge management.

Once a strategy for a business unit is selected and the scope for knowledge management solution is determined, then the planning phase begins.

Now, let us deep dive into various knowledge management environments where KM systems might come into existence:

1. KNOWLEDGE MANAGEMENT STAND-ALONE SYSTEMS

Here, KM systems could be built by one or two individuals as a self-initiative or self-motivated at the project level, program level or any of the knowledge entities based on certain knowledge needs.

The developed KM initiatives may not necessarily be enterprise-driven and may not even be necessarily from KM function or central KM teams. It can even exist in organizations where there might not be any formal KM.

The result of such standalone KMS is healthy offshoots in the organizations. In such a scenario, you can easily plan to integrate other requirements from ISO 30401 and have a functional KMS system as per the standard locally.

This could eventually lead to organizations setting up full-fledged KM functions too. The organization must take into account such offshoots, develop similar KM programs in the organization and broad-base the use of KM solutions at that organization level.

2. ORGANIZATIONS MEDIUM/LARGE SIZE

When it comes to large and mid-size organizations, getting the right KM solution could be complicated without effective planning.

The KM function needs to develop a KM strategy that is aligned to corporate strategy. Having zero downed on the Knowledge proximity orders and selecting the primary interested parties, the planning should happen along with the stakeholders and HR/training/Business Leaders to develop KM architecture holistically and deriving the KM roadmap.

You will have to capture the entire organization's Knowledge Proximity matrix and map out the entire knowledge flows and structures, i.e. map the existing formal KM of Knowledge exchange and explicit knowledge. Then zero down on the interests, party's requirement and develop the KM roadmap.

Once the KM requirement blueprint is drafted, the team can look at various gaps, discuss with the business leaders, come up with the detailed knowledge domain requirements, which we saw in the KMS generic case.

Here, we will cover this aspect in a much detailed way. It is important to ask these primary questions and take inference from these questions, the direction and narrative of the planning:

- What is the KM strategy for the organization?
- What are various KM entities?
- What should be the strategy to assess requirements?
- What should be the tactical way of handling it?

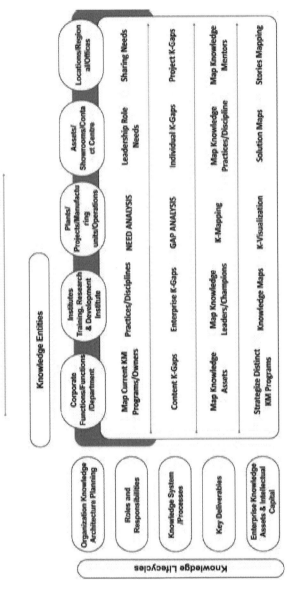

Diagram K.M.A.P.S 1 – KM Architecture Planning Schema Illustration

- How do you develop KM technology solutions?
- How do you have the right people doing the KM function?
- What kind of skills, competency, experiences is needed to fit the development of the KM ecosystem?
- What kind of environment does the management need to develop to establish KM culture?
- What kind of investment is required to establish a full-fledged KM function and associated technologies?
- How many FTEs (Full-time employees) are needed to drive KM in this form at the strategic level?

Then based on the chosen areas, the business leader needs to look at tactically how to address the challenges. These challenges could be:

- What are the business challenges at hand?
- What are the available KM solutions?
- Do IT-KM systems need customization?
- Does it meet the needed out-of-the-box configuration?
- How do we develop taxonomy for the business unit to manage critical knowledge assets, process assets, expertise mapping, and build communities and conversations to mentor and guide?
- How to plan the implementation of KMs?
- What are the challenges or pitfalls of implementing this program to all the knowledge management tools?
- What strategy to device to overcome these pitfalls?

- How to energize the project leadership, product team managers in this process of development, then what are their needs at that level?

- And what are the challenges in terms of the knowledge domain?

The planning should also include different services, functions and should engage the function department working in certain units or business lines.

- How do you plan their mutual collaboration mechanism?

- What are the challenges, how to overcome these challenges?

- What are the catalysts who are the catalysts who could provide the guidance and lead in a business bind?

- What are the key demands?

- How can they build the support teams, supporting the initiative?

- How can they develop people who want to contribute to this initiative?

- What are the needs? How do you capture the needs?

- How to create the KMs solutions catalogue?

- How to develop the technology of KM practices based on KM practices for non-tech people, tech-people?

- How to develop procedures and manuals for the users when it comes to project or the grass-root level, there need to be other plans in place, exams, communication plan, change management plan, people engagement plan, etc.?

Some of these points have been covered in strategic tactical planning. Now you need to understand how to go about actually doing things on the ground. That is how we do operationalize knowledge management on the ground.

If knowledge management technology needs to create a KM project plan to get the whole schedule created with the resource loaded and other communication sorted out, these are the questions that must be considered:

- Why launch KM?
- How do you launch the KM system?
- Who is your primary audience?
- What communication do you plan to send?
- What is that, I mean, what design elements are you going to use?
- How are you going to develop manuals and documentation for usage? What are the other KM practices being defined?
- How to nominate experts for knowledge sharing?
- How many usable artifacts should have been contributed? How many knowledge assets I should have contributed? Learn how many mentees need to be trained? How to groom and train the rookies? Who are the experts? That in point, what level of expert competency and skills they need to be trained in?
- What are the key lessons being shared, and when do they need to share?
- How are the teams supposed to communicate updates within the team, external to the team and vice versa?

- How can leaders manage solid leads that everybody knows within the team?
- How do you encourage the team to call the higher management to celebrate success?
- What are the Rewards and Recognition[72] devised?
- What are the Reward and Recognition given for the highest KM value generators, and how do you provide encouragement to knowledge consumers?
- How many publications or what newsletters or content cards are the teams supposed to be provided, etc.?

It is also important for KM function and management to plan on:

1. How to develop KPIs[73] on the metrics?
2. How to capture the effectiveness of KM system practices in the KM function?
3. How to capture the data point, pints of the number of case studies, best practices, IPs, patents, frameworks, guides, updates, communication, newsletter, knowledge assets, Communities of Practice, LL workshops, peer-to-peer workshops?
4. How do you capture the voice of customers and make it to the dashboard?
5. How do you get feedback on KM practices and develop it?

There are a few planning elements when it comes to governance. There are aspects of KPIs for government entities, academics, Institutes, product manufacturers and product development, and startups.

What is important is that we need to use these metrics as indicators of the progress made in the KM journey, rather than using them as target numbers and changing the context of managing knowledge to managing numbers.

You can also use the below KMS Design Reference Tenets to plan and design a knowledge management system.

Overall, there should be at least five years of strategic planning with KM blueprint and road map. If you are starting afresh; the management should have a two-year tactical plan and a yearly operational plan. You can develop further communication, engagement and learning plans to manage the KM program well.

Knowledge Management System Design Tenants

01 Initiate	02 Plan	03 Design	04 Implement	05 Operation	06 Continuous Improvement

Leadership
Governance
KM Culture
KM Process
KM Technology and Infrastructure
KMS Policy and Documentation
KM Content
People's Role and Structure
Communication Management
KM Program/Initiative Management
KM Support
KM Operation

Diagram – K.M.D.T 1 – KMS Design Tenants

CHAPTER EIGHT

KNOWLEDGE DEVELOPMENT PROCESS

In this chapter, we are going to scuba-dive into **knowledge management development**. In the previous chapters, we learned about the entire process in its natural flow of working while executing the KM initiative.

Now, let's look at the various processes that are essential for knowledge development in any knowledge entity. There are 4 core processes[74] that form the complete cycle of KM.

1. Acquiring new knowledge,
2. Applying existing knowledge,
3. Retaining knowledge
4. Handling outdated knowledge.

If we go back to the marketing and sales function perspective; when it comes to acquiring knowledge, the marketing team should learn from the customers, feedback on new product knowledge, market reactions on the new products, insights on competition, etc. This knowledge on the ground level would help to manage the customer's expectations and learn about the dealing strength by talking about the features, etc.

When it comes to applying Knowledge, it is very important for the team to gather all the knowledge needed about the product from the repositories, asking questions about the updates and other queries to seniors or product development managers. This would ensure they are on top of their trade and maximize the experience of the customer to benefit the usage of the product. This would also provide holistic details, information on everything that a customer wants to hear and make decisions to clock order. Few in the team might need various forms of presentations, material templates, and other artifacts to prepare presentations, sales pitches and case studies for the client visit. And if they are new joiners, then you also need to get them on board.

So within the team, there could be an expert sharing session about the experience of marketing and selling to the client. They can create how-to videos about learning and can have a mentorship kind of channel where they could mentor the rookies or fresh graduates, et cetera.

Now, at the end of this knowledge cycle, a new clarity in all the marketing functions emerges. It is also necessary that as new products are introduced, the information should be updated. I mean, there are old products that are being discontinued from the product catalog. So, all the contents related to the old product have to be purged or archived out of the digital spaces, that is portals, websites, links, etc. It is also important for the people moving out to have an important session; Knowledge Transfer Session[75] plan. The people who are moving out might have published success stories based on the experts, making great sales or marketing in the area of the organization.

So as you see, most of the processes are examples with respect to knowledge development stages from the perspective of knowledge entity marketing and sales function. The prototype of the system helps in streamlining the learning capabilities, connecting mentors with mentees, connecting people with content are all various aspects of acquiring, applying, retaining and handling outdated knowledge when it comes to KM cycles in the marketing and sales department

The idea here from the standard point of view is, an organization is able to view the knowledge life cycle in its entirety and they are able to develop the solution at every stage.

When you speak of a knowledge entity, you must consider what kind of knowledge are you referring to, if you are able to develop a knowledge entity matrix, or you could also refer to the knowledge development[44] framework. So these would provide more information on the entire knowledge cycle of a particular knowledge entity.

I would like to share one important learning about planning KM. That is, the knowledge needs of a specific audience do not remain constant. From what I have learned, when certain services are provided with regard to knowledge needs, that becomes the baseline of Knowledge fulfillment, and this requirement continuously grows with business users. It is important to remember this and document any new requirement as and when it arises. It could be documented as informal feedback, criticism, opinions, everyday conversation, or formal tracking.

This provides a glimpse of the knowledge development cycle with respect to a specific knowledge entity, now there are various methods and approaches which have to be carefully planned and designed as per the KM system tenets so that every aspect of it is addressed to effectively manage knowledge across the lifecycle. Let's learn more about this in the next chapter which is aligned with ISO 30401 KMS.

CHAPTER NINE
KNOWLEDGE CONVEYANCE AND TRANSFORMATION

Now, we are going to briefly look at various knowledge conveyance, transformational[76] tools and techniques offered in the KM field.

As discussed in an earlier chapter, when it comes to KM solutions after the initial design phase designing the knowledge circles, knowledge needs order identification, mapping the existing knowledge landscape, the organization needs to carefully craft the KM solutions. It could be practice-oriented, IT system-oriented, or it could be hybrid i.e. mix of classic KM with IT Tools and developing practices around the cultural aspects. Please refer to the Appendix for a detailed Clause mapping template.

Based on the layers of knowledge flow, the requirement gaps are developed and the KM solution is designed and implemented. Again, there are certain questions that should be answered:

- What are the various KM tools and Methods? Why to use these methods and tools?
- Does it need deep cultural Change management?
- Are interventions needed to bring together teams and do community learning?
- Does the team spend too much time searching for valid content and face difficulty in finding them?
- Is the team finding the communications thwarted when it comes to New product updates etc.?
- Is the learning, sharing not happening between two projects, two functions, multiple team members?
- Is the tacit experience of teams not captured effectively for organizational dissemination?
- Is the feedback from the market and customers not able to develop competitive intelligence?
- So on and so forth

Each of these problem statements would lead to opt for various KM solutions which include various methods, tools, and practices. This book will not dwell on the KM solutions per se but provides a list of some of the KM techniques and solutions broadly used across the globe and it is not an exhaustive list. Again the importance here is the utilization of as many possible methods as possible to create results and solve knowledge problems.

Identifying the knowledge
- Knowledge Assessment Tool
- Knowledge Café
- Communities of Practice
- Advanced Search Tools
- Building Knowledge Clusters
- Expertise Locator/Who's Who
- Collaborative Virtual Workspaces
- Knowledge Mapping
- K Maturity Model
- Mentor/Mentee Scheme

Creating Knowledge
- Brainstorming
- Learnings and Ideas Capture
- Learning Reviews
- After Action Reviews
- Collaborative Physical Workspaces
- Knowledge Café
- Communities of Practice
- Knowledge Bases (Wikis, etc.) Blogs
- Video Communication and Webinars
- Advanced Search Building
- Knowledge Clusters
- Expertise Locator/Who's Who
- Collaborative Virtual Workspaces
- Mentor/Mentee Scheme
- Knowledge Portal
- Peer Sharing

Storing knowledge
- Learning Reviews
- After Action Reviews
- Collaborative Physical Workspaces
- Knowledge Café
- Communities of Practice
- Knowledge Bases (Wikis, etc.) Blogs
- Video Communication and Webinars
- Advanced Search
- Building Knowledge Clusters
- Expertise Locator/Who's Who
- Collaborative Virtual Workspaces Mentor/Mentee Scheme Knowledge Portal
- Video Sharing

Sharing knowledge
- Peer Assist
- Learning Reviews After Action Reviews
- Storytelling
- Collaborative Physical Workspaces 09. Knowledge Café
- Communities of Practice
- Document Libraries
- Knowledge Bases (Wikis, etc.)
- Social Network Services
- Video Communication and Webinars
- Building Knowledge Clusters
- Expertise Locator/Who's Who
- Collaborative Virtual Workspaces Knowledge Portal Video Sharing Mentor/Mentee Scheme
- Blogs

Applying Knowledge
- Peer Assist
- Collaborative Physical Workspaces
- Knowledge Café
- Communities of Practice
- Document Libraries
- Knowledge Bases (Wikis, etc.)
- Blogs
- Video Communication and Webinars
- Advanced Search
- Building Knowledge Clusters
- Expertise Locator/Who's Who
- Collaborative Virtual Workspaces
- Knowledge Portal
- Knowledge Worker Competency Plan
- Mentor/Mentee Scheme

Classic KM Methods
- Brainstorming
- Learnings and Ideas Capture
- Peer Assist
- Learning Reviews
- After Action Review
- Storytelling
- Collaborative Physical Workspaces
- Knowledge Assessments
- Knowledge Café
- Communities of Practice

IT KM Systems
- Cloud Computing
- Document Management system
- Record Management System
- Knowledge Bases (Wikis, etc.)
- Social Network Services
- Video Communication and Webinars
- Advanced Search Tools
- Building Knowledge Clusters
- Expertise Locator/Who's Who 20. Collaborative Virtual Workspaces

Diagram K.M.S.M.T I.-1- KMS Methods and Tools list (Adopted from ADB's Knowledge Solution [77])

CHAPTER TEN

KNOWLEDGE ENABLERS

In this chapter, we will learn about **knowledge management enablers.** When the knowledge interaction happens between various knowledge entities, the central to it is human or individual and his/her knowledge landscape becomes pivotal to every aspect of management of knowledge[78].

If you take, for example, the knowledge circle and the various knowledge needs order assembled the roles of people.

And to assemble this required knowledge in the domain of physical, social or digital or any other dimensions[79], it needs technology, people performing various roles require social interaction needs physical/electrical/electronic infrastructure. And to manage the entire lifecycle-governance is very important.

In the above example, we saw how the organization implemented a knowledge management system. However, to make it successful, there are several enablers involved:

1. People
2. Process
3. Technology

4. Culture

5. Governance

PEOPLE

KM happens at the human-centric level.

In large organizations, there should be dedicated people who could work with stakeholders, appraise the existing gaps in the knowledge flow in its entire knowledge cycle. So, KM function, in general, can consist of at least one person to start with and continue to grow based on the size and capacity of the organization. This can build a strong KM function based on the breadth of the organizational KM and its requirement over a period of time.

If an organization is a small or medium-scale or Startup, there could be one person playing multiple roles. It is important to find that person who is analytic, introspective, practical, empathetic, to understand other member's knowledge needs, their knowledge challenges, and add value in building classic and technology-based KM solutions to help in setting up out-of-the-box KMS or KMS stand-alone.

KM function becomes central to the large MNCs. However, it doesn't stop KM functions to create an army of KM volunteers, champions in their own field so that they can participate and contribute in knowledge work, i.e. to manage the acquired/created/reused/purged knowledge wherever they are working.

PROCESS

When the KM system was launched in a previous example, there were several outcomes of the exercise:

1. Training material and how to create awareness,
2. Procedure-
    a. Procedure of how to use the portal example,
    b. Procedure of how to upload the content,
    c. Procedure of how to approve the content,
    d. Who approves,
    e. When to approve the timeline within, and
    f. What has to be approved.

   There are a lot of other documented processes that must be aligned to the business outcome.

3. Methods-
    a. Provide overall document on how to utilize the assets,
    b. How to create knowledge assets; quality K-Assets, at what juncture are the assets required to be created and uploaded in the repository?

4. Measurement- The team also added on how to measure the Knowledge assets, KPI in terms of how many assets have been added, how many were downloaded and the effectiveness of reuse. It is part of monthly tasks and many other tasks that a marketing team performs.

5. Knowledge Sharing - Sales agents learn from winning calls during the day shift or share the winning strategy with the team in a knowledge sharing session or write stories to communicate with other members of the team. It is a great way of nurturing the knowledge exchange within the team and across

if it is interwoven in their personal performance indicators or the yearly objectives.

It could also be made a part of the work instruction embedded in the standard operating procedure.

There are a few categories of the processes to be aware of:

1. Processes on developing KM Framework at the highest level

2. Processes on KM system lifecycle management

3. Processes on KM development process- creation, development, reuse, archival supporting activities with respect to KM systems

4. KM Processes being embedded in the business process as a checklist or mandatory requirements depending on the severity of the knowledge process

5. Processes to measure, evaluate and improve the KM systems

TECHNOLOGY

The next enabler is technology and infrastructure as discussed earlier. When it comes to managing and distilling knowledge in the digital form in computing, mobile devices, et cetera, technology in the field of KM has advanced extensively. Therefore, every organization spends a great number of resources, effort and time developing it.

Organizations that do not want to develop homegrown solutions from scratch have cloud-based KM solutions in the market, which could be licensed depending on the user license. These solutions can be deployed on a large scale and reduce the initial investment.

There are various free online systems as well as which can be used by various small or medium enterprises If cost is the barrier.

In the marketing KM case, we saw how the knowledge portal, people profile and lessons learned system were deployed in the marketing team. If the technology is at the forefront of today's work from home, office, our work product environment tools then the workspace, all content, data records, information line of business, content apps, content website are all in the digital/virtual domain. The technology had superimposed on the KM till recently.

Technology infrastructure is one of the important enablers. When we talk about work infrastructure, there are other forms and formats required for knowledge management, training centers, online training, conference hall, meeting halls, knowledge infrastructure[80] to organize knowledge jams and conferences, knowledge cafes, knowledge fairs, workshops, seminars, peer review sessions, etc.

Infrastructure can also encompass various futuristic technologies like robotics, Artificial-intelligence-based systems[81], augmented reality[82]. We might need separate volumes of this book to talk about various KM technologies and systems as it's not possible to cover them in this book.

However, it is essential to have technology at the heart of the needs of Knowledge workers in the organization, so that it can support digital transformation in other levels where knowledge is also managed.

This is how I see a few categories of KM Technology and Infrastructure:

1. Generic KM

2. Classic KM

3. Advanced KM

4. Futuristic KM

Generic KM – In generic KM, some of the principles are already integrated into training, HR, IT department driving, learning, competency management and various other portal solutions. They might not be tagged or driven by KM function, however, they are an important part of KM functioning in the organization.

Classic KM – There are organizations that have cleverly defined robust execution, operational and are productive, excellence-driven. They have knowledge management more like a traditional method of mentor-mentee concept, seniors training the juniors over a period of time, getting interns to work under professionals to learn from their direct experience. There are even organizations that encourage rich conversation, people-to-people connect, and have less use of digital mediums for communication and knowledge sharing. These companies as well might have strong roots in KM principles. And these practices could be creating a major impact on the outcomes.

Ex: Just-in-time, 5S[83], QMS, etc.

Advanced KM – Organizations invest in KM technologies to develop KM architecture and offer KM-IT services within and outside the organizations. It is labeled as advanced KM because of its multiple paradigms, resources requirement, systematic way of approaching things and solving business challenges by using digital KM solutions[84]. And these systems become essential to sustain geographical connectivity and collaboration, like now the collaboration technology is inevitable.

Futuristic KM – When an organization has established classic, advanced KM and can see significant operational and productive excellence, then the company will be ready to invest in emerging research-based technology and experiment to create a new 360-degree experience of KM like augmentation[85], knowledge visualization[86] and projected Knowledge spheres, etc.

GOVERNANCE

Let's learn about governance in the primary control systems to manage and monitor the entire KMS Functions or initiatives. In the last case, we saw how governance encompasses a broad array associated with leadership, planning, resources, documentation, operation, and people. So, when we talk about KM leadership, we refer to developing KM procedures, KM policies, developing KM reporting structure, developing measurement & outcomes, and management of KM function.

Governance could be achieved in multiple ways; as the KM function grows and encompasses the entire organization, the large organization could be different from smaller organizations.

You could split into multiple categories where you have a knowledge management system as:

- Ad-Hoc KM principles-based initiatives from various Functions under various labels

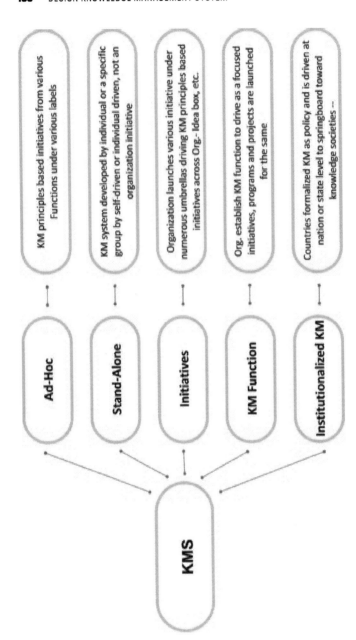

Diagram K.E.C 1 - KMS Existence Category

- Stand-alone - KM system developed by an individual or a specific group by self-driven or individual-driven, not an organization initiative

- KM initiatives - The organization launches various initiatives under numerous umbrellas, driving KM principles-based initiatives across the organization-Idea box, etc.

- Knowledge Management System driven by KM function - Organizations establish KM function to drive as focused initiatives, programs and projects are launched for the same

- KM Driven Nationally - Countries formalize KM as policy and is driven at the nation or state level to springboard toward knowledge societies[87]

So, when it comes to KMS stand-alone, security management and procedures at the local level are important. The same needs to be defined wherever the ad-hoc initiatives are operational in the organization.

But when it comes to KMS as a function; a security management procedure, policy, KPI management reviews, various other forms of documentation and the execution of KM has to be managed well. And if the organization is going for certification, they also need to go with external and internal audits.

KMS governance can be achieved in multiple ways as the KM function grows.

The organization could be a:

A large organization with multiple clients,

A large organization with multiple accounts,

A large organization with multiple engineering projects,

A large organization with multiple products,

A large organization with multiple locations or business units, or

A large organization with multiple services.

Each of these organizations needs to develop governance, according to the extent of the KM drive and in intended reach within the organization.

For example, in the previous case, if the marketing team has to launch a KM initiative, this would be one subset of the organization level KM, or it could be an initiative and the function level or the business unit level.

Let me share some *strategic ways of managing KM in large organizations*[88].

KM function can have multiple KM programs and you can have multiple KM portfolios Under each of these portfolios, there could be multiple projects and programs, of a similar kind or the same project depending on how you define the KM Management.

However, if it is client-based knowledge management, the initiative has multiple methods and systems, all this could be managed under one KM program umbrella.

Secondly, we can do it as a scheme of portfolios, a hard set of KM projects and other KM programs. KM project for a specific client or KM solutions could be categorized as the KM program, which doesn't have a specific end date. For example, how we manage the repository in the program after launching as it has no end date. So, this whole aspect could be a program within a portfolio.

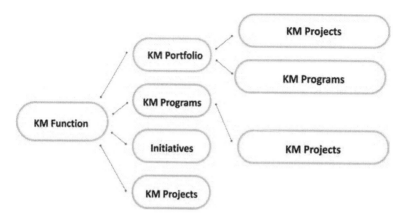

Diagram K.M.F.S 1 – KM function Structures example

The Enterprise-driven KM could have a steering committee as the executive sponsor for the KM function. The KM function ideally should be under the Corporate strategy/ organizational development department.

This way, it will have complete access to the management and ease to drive the KM strategically. It also needs to have the KM Business working group, whose responsibility is to provide the business rules and architecture for the KM function in such a way that the KM solutions are developed in a holistic fashion.

The KM function can drive the entire KM services, support and operations from design to managing to implementation of KM systems and reporting to the chairing business sponsor working group/committee.

The KM Steering committee is the one that approves the budget, scoping and formalization of knowledge management, vision and mission along with the business sponsor working group.

KM functions along with the business working group's inputs and the guidelines could develop KM roadmaps, KM plans, guidelines for the business, initiate KM projects, establish KM programs in the organization.

KM PROGRAMS

KM programs could be focused on providing KM solutions to clients, functions, departments, service lines or business lines. The program could be started to initiate long-term engagement; for example, managing KM repositories, sustaining communities, organize and manage regular KM exchange initiatives like calendared sessions from experts, case studies, best practices programs, etc.

The KM programs should be a very focused approach from the KM functions, these could have KM system development project and content management program for the same knowledge entities.

KM PROGRAMS ON KM TECHNOLOGY

- Large multiple projects to build a KM technology based on systems.
- Integrated with KM services support with KM function set as a self-service module.
- Support team management of users, part of one of the programs locally and globally.

KM Initiatives based on themes, like short-term-focused drive should be targeted:

- to drive the collection of reusable content, modules software,
- to collect ideas, case studies, best practices.

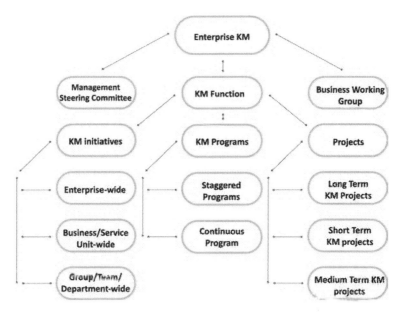

Diagram -E.K.M.I.S 1- Enterprise KM Implementation Structure Example

Now, let's look at the KM function.

What would comprise a KM function?

KM function needs to have KM technologies, taxonomist, knowledge analyst, program management, KM content management. The details have been covered in Chapter 11: Support (under the heading Competencies).

And at every business level, there is a need to have a KM champion, KM leaders, business leaders who know the domain and are functional experts in their field.

We also need a technology team with Software developers, administration analyst, based on the technology needs.

Then there's a requirement of communication and change management personnel who are responsible for writing the content, managing the content quality, graphic design communication manager, et cetera.

There should be a working committee to decide on the scope. These could be the domain experts or functional experts at the business unit. Service unit heads should become a part of this committee to sponsor and drive their KM in their business/service/functional units to make it full-fledged implemented and supported to make it effective

The above-mentioned members for the KM function are a sample indication of the composition of the KM function team for a very large organization. However, when it comes to small and medium enterprises, the number of KM personal requirements could differ and can start with a small team that can play multiple roles as and when required. It is entirely up to the organization, its constraints and availability of budgets.

Now, these sets of personals are very much important as the KM function.

And according to my experience, each of the roles mentioned can be performed by any individual with enthusiasm and proactiveness to make a difference in the knowledge domain in their field. It needs a little extra effort from individuals to perform activities and tasks, which are added along with their day-to-day operations.

The KM could be integrated into individual KPIs or performance targets for the year.

To develop effective governance on documentation, the following needs to be considered:

- Governance is top-down driven, essentially it needs to be aligned with the Knowledge roles, as the knowledge worker needs to understand his role and provide feedback to the related parties to develop robust KM processes.

- Governance, though is important, but it should not become itself a barrier in knowledge sharing.

- Governance is critical, it needs to abided by law of the land, the policy of the organization and industry guidelines.

- The governance framework should be designed from the grass-root level to fit in the local culture and organizational culture aspect too, as this is going to provide better engagement of users with regard to the system of KM.

Note: Over security or over scrutiny or a thick level of protection could lead KMs into a pitfall.

- We need to remember that KM is not about policing, but the creation of the environment, which we will deep-dive into in the upcoming KM Culture section.

- The common KM policy should be developed at the enterprise level, next, at the regional level and the local level.

KM CULTURE

When the KM repository is launched with the marketing team, there are various scenarios at play based on the:

1. KM system designed without the team's involvement

2. KM system designed with the team's involvement

1. KM system designed without the team's involvement:

When the system is designed outside the user community involvement, management makes it mandatory for the teams to use it.

The marketing group might start updating non-important documents, just to showcase that they are contributing and trying to persuade the management that the tool is not good enough for various reasons. And this can be greatly detrimental to the whole KM effectiveness, and eventually, lead to failure of the systems.

When the knowledge management system gets launched without the engagement of existing users, most people think this tool is not user-friendly.

And there is a certain category of people who will hate the idea of the KM system as their self-importance would be lost. They would do all the things in their power to not upload the crucial documents and retain the critical role they play in the working of teams. People do not want to disclose all their learnings and insights to the team so easily.

It means, in the next six to ten months, when the management becomes busy with some other areas of business, the team slowly goes back to the old ways of working. Then one day, the management finds that this KMs system is not being used and there's no usage or engagement from the user. They try to convince people to use it. By this time, the group would have formed a strong opinion and conscious agreement not to use the tool. This is how a KM system fails.

This is also one of the reasons why most of the technology-oriented KMs have failed miserably in the past as the organization believed that getting a KM technology will solve the knowledge challenges. This illusion also got busted in recent years and the classic KM has emerged much stronger. With the release of the first ISO standard, it has given greater impetus to the classic KM and then to evolve the KM practices and technology being just one of the enablers.

It shows that technology is only one spoke of the entire wheel with very many other spokes.

2. KM system designed with the team's involvement

The other scenario which could play in the team's behavior is when they are involved from the initial stage.

They need to be engaged very closely from the time of Initiation to the Implementation stage of the KM system. When the team is involved in the complete life cycle of the design of the KM system, it becomes convenient for the team to see and provide feedback and inputs on their requirements and develop KM in agile mode. This way, their concerns get resolved, this also leads to IA architecture, search design, security features are incorporated as per their work activities or work sets. It would act as a complement to the job function rather than obstructing their flow of work activity.

When launched, most of the team will embrace it.

And also people who were actively engaged in the envisioning workshops and KM champions would propagate the KM system and its usage. The feeling "not from here syndrome" will not exist within the social space of the team; the acceptance and management of content become much faster. It becomes a part of their daily work activities. So active engagement is essential for the KM team or the team-in-charge of KM design or people across the department, home, the team it has been catered to.

As we saw above, organizations need to engage employees especially when it comes to Knowledge Management.

Here are some of the important points to be considered:

- Understand the concern and develop a user-centered KM system, and design processes as per the taskonomy.

- From the Initiation stage to the Development stage to the Launch and Operation phase of the KM tool, there has to be continuous engagement and communication in terms of what is expected from the KM project or initiative, what is expected at the end of this development.

- The team needs to be trained and awareness has to be created multiple times, reaching out to the entire user base, where they can further explain to their secondary audience.

- Leadership management can focus on R&D and process integration rather than selling the tool.

- As the KM leader, it's important to manage the team's knowledge and processes. The systems have to be established in cognizant with the user. This is the most important aspect of KM culture.

SPHERE OF PSYCHOLOGY

The complexity has already been explained in the world of knowledge and how humans have to switch between multiple domains every day, day in and day out.

Our brains are getting acquainted with new forms of mediums, new paths to knowledge in various dimensions. Nowhere in the past, man was subjugated with such vastitude and the flux of the digital content, media streams, digital paths, multiple domains. For example:

There is a need for so much to be remembered at one time, which an average human is incapable of handling in his personal life.

In the past, they haven't had to remember so much to survive in their jobs. Normally, the stress on the mental capabilities had too much stuff to process in alignment with the pressing demands in the jobs. Especially, this Digital world has flattened the whole globe and has amplified the rate at which knowledge flows. The velocity of knowledge is mind-blowing and tires the human mind.

An average man should upskill his business skills and display experience of gratitude, creating results.

He needs to hold on to his ground to show that he is very important in the line of his work. It is important to meet the organization's goal to extend employability and manage the growth and progression in the career, which is directly linked to one's capability.

It is important to know that every individual is doing every important thing by being committed to his growth and progress.

As survival will depend on this context, there is a large number of people who may belong to this group, or they may be working just to get through life.

The KM work is not just a mainstream source of revenue, but there are other things in life supporting them too. I have dealt with individuals from many backgrounds, different nationalities and belief systems. Respecting Personal cultural background and acknowledgement of their expertise are important to invoke a common trait of loyalty.

This is again a very important leadership trait that needs to be managed to drive the knowledge management culture. The leaders or managers can create this kind of common interest and motivate the team. It is essential to develop the foundation of greater collaboration and group activity.

CHAPTER ELEVEN

SUPPORT

The management needs to evaluate the requirements of the knowledge management system and provide all the needed funding, infrastructure, management support, full-time employees[89] in order to manage the entire life cycle of knowledge management.

Again, when it comes to knowledge management requirements, there are multiple aspects to it. Let's review some of the salient requirements:

1. Does the organization have a budget for KM function, system and team?

2. Will the management drive KM culture and steer the program?

3. Does the person chosen to facilitate knowledge management design understands the industry-standard technology, business, people, and has management support?

4. Do you have the tools, methodology, framework, approaches, and way of doing things to facilitate the knowledge sharing, knowledge creation, knowledge

reuse, harvesting, and knowledge archiving processes, methods in place?

5. Do you have people who would create, develop the KM practices as a way of life in this transactional corporate world?

These are some of the important KM rules to be followed by the business solution leaders in the context of enterprise or corporate or large-scale knowledge management deployment. However, even the small and medium-scale industries would want to implement KMS, it can work on resources and can scale it up.

Here are a few rules that must be considered:

- Do you have people driving the KM Initiative?
- What support do they need?
- What resources do they need?
- Teach them the KM principles and create an eco-system to develop knowledge management solutions with classical methods and technology-oriented practices.

When it comes to KMS standalone system resources, one can use custom-developed simple intranets to develop effective knowledge management. And if this works for a small firm, it can be evolved further, processes can be created around KMS and KMS can be aligned to the standard requirements.

When we speak about resources, these are closely tied to the KM practices: what we are going to adopt.

For example, in this case of knowledge asset management, the resources required could be non-IT resources, workshops with the team, Excel sheets, Post-its, paper, pencils, design workshops, etc.

Project resource loading may include, for example, the various activities that are going to be performed, how many resources are needed, how many man-hours are needed, so this generally shows the resource loading for a particular activity.

COMPETENCIES

This involves KM functions in an organization, or the KM function departments, or the KM-based standalone roles. If it's being sponsored by the organization, first of all, the leadership team needs to find the right people for the KM function or KM-based role. The following questions are the most important way to analyze the leadership level:

- Does the person who is going to lead KM has previous experience in the KM domain or has the ability to lead?

- Does he have the flare to understand the business context and deliver results appropriately?

- What are the success rates in past? What documentation can prove his capabilities and experience? Does he have experience in managing programs, teams, technologies, KM solutions?

There are areas where many KM failures have happened not because of the KM leader; but because the business function did not understand the vastness and depth of knowledge management.

Therefore, it is important and very much critical that business leaders understand the holistic nature of KM and step outside the conventional and trend-based KM. Instead, knowledge management can't happen from outside; it needs to start within the organization. It has to be started by the experts, by the heads, by the managers. They become the locus of developing effective KM culture and solutions.

Technology is just an extension of the need-fulfillment. If the KM needs and its cycle are identified, it gives a greater dimension to deal with it.

For example: When we talk about human potential, human wellbeing, we are setting multiple contexts of human domains. Like there are multiple systems to make the human body function[90] from birth to death - nervous system, respiratory system, digestive system and so on. Similarly, when we talk about an organization with KM, there are multiple dimensions in terms of the knowledge management systems to work on.

We can consider our organization as an intelligent social system. Are the processes of standardization, the body of knowledge in alignment with the line of business? Organizational knowledge management system could develop into effective intelligent social systems[91], charting new paths to beat the market, having innovation eco-system aligned to social, market needs.

Now, coming back to resources, it varies from different KMS environmental context. So, what are the resources that should be used?

GROUP/PROJECT/INDIVIDUAL LEVEL KM

When it comes to the individual level:

- there are multiple document management systems,

- reusable assets., How-to's, body of knowledge, process and knowledge repositories, business rules know-hows, etc.

- record management systems,

- collaboration spaces, which could be used for telegrams,

- developing individual or group taxonomies based on the area of disciplines or topics of discipline, activities, lifecycle, other aspects of work, work product, collaboration work products,

- how are the internal-external links managed?

- are the experts listed and profiled?

- get the expert on LinkedIn and get learning solutions.

For individual knowledge management, one needs to fulfill work with data and ask for the required information.

Generally, an individual fulfills his knowledge either by asking a colleague, asking the manager, asking the experts, searching the web or asking anybody in that field. If not, escalate what is the piece of information that is missing. This gap in terms of finding the information, communication gaps and document gaps, is primary for knowledge management.

Escalate the knowledge needs of the team or the person-in-charge of knowledge management[92]. This would provide impetus to the next level of knowledge management evolution of missing content or missing data.

Now, let's review the key points to be considered at the individual psychological level:

- What if your organization does not have a formal KM?

- It is important to think about what if you are enveloped in challenges, receiving critical documents?
- Why does my team need to request multiple times and follow up with the same information requirement every month?
- How do I perform this task?
- How do I perform this activity?
- How do I ask, "Where are these application links?" I am not able to find the digital format.
- How to ask my manager? He always thinks that I am misrepresenting the document.
- How do I ask this question to any of my colleagues? They would think "I don't know anything."
- How do I find relevant experiential knowledge in this work area management? Who can help?

So, it is very important to understand the circle of knowledge cycle and fulfill one's knowledge needs by developing an individual knowledge management system, team knowledge management system, so on and so forth. This is one of the primary competencies. Whether it's individual at the business or project level, one has to fulfill one's own knowledge requirements. At the organizational level, one has to fulfill the knowledge requirements of the organization.

KMS STAND-ALONE

These are essentially people-driven practices:

- These are zero-budget or very low-cost KM initiatives. The KM uses existing resources, people-incentive programs, and social engagement.

- Resources required are more in terms of extensive communication in an organization. It requires critical facilitation, large groups, workshops, peer-to-peer group discussions.

ENTERPRISE KM

We are looking at internal knowledge management at the enterprise level:

- What are the KM digital systems?
- Does your organization have a knowledge management expert or analyst?
- It also requires the KM technology team.
- It also needs knowledge management infrastructure like meeting rooms, conference rooms, auditoriums, knowledge-sharing jamming spaces, and various other support infrastructures.
- Budgets could vary from high budget to low budgets and R&Rs (Rewards and Recognition).

This initial investment in technology would be high in the initial phase but if you use the cloud-based technology, the initial investment could be lower. However, the pros and cons need to be understood. It is also important to integrate knowledge visualization rooms with Augmented Reality (AR).

NATIONAL KM

How do you roll out knowledge management nationwide?

You will have to create:

- knowledge-management units,

- center of excellence for knowledge and innovation,
- facilitation experts,
- develop facilitation infrastructures,
- facilitation materials, software mapping, database mapping,
- list of all key stakeholders in the industry, a list of professional bodies, a list of institutes, a list of government entities, a list of key personals,
- set up Knowledge Discovery workshop,
- set up communication boards, pinup boards to put up strategies, tactics and operations; plan everything on board.

With this, the first year starts with the basics:

- Spend time mapping, involve people, try and get the right team, get the right stakeholders.
- Create a blueprint at the highest level. Take one prototype, one grass-root level at the same time, and show results.
- Write communications, provide outcome expectations.
- Provide a communication framework.
- Prepare a list of work products.
- Prepare activity sets.
- Prepare task sets.
- Prepare the KMO dashboard.
- Prepare communication packages.
- Prepare KM systems, process guidelines, templates, mailers, meetings, role empowerment, R&R.

At the national level[93], different Continents[94, 95], different individual knowledge entities need to find the local and global knowledge requirements and develop Knowledge management at every level of human existence[96, 97,] . Ex: Healthcare, Natural Disaster, Industry best practices, Agriculture Development[98, 99], cross-collaboration, etc.

KM COMPETENCY DEVELOPMENT

This is something very rudimentary when it comes to knowledge management. On several occasions, I have been asked by multiple people, "How to become a knowledge manager?" My answer has always been, "It depends." Broadly, based on my experience, after observing various organizations, I have worked with, dozens of clients with whom I have built the knowledge management system, I have got a fair understanding of KM.

Here are a few critical skills/competencies that will lay the path:

1. knowledge management, a technical path,

2. facilitation, knowledge management path,

3. content, knowledge management path,

4. program management, knowledge management path,

5. support, knowledge management path,

6. research and innovation, knowledge management path,

7. change management communication specialist, knowledge management path.

TECHNICAL PATH IN KNOWLEDGE MANAGEMENT

Now, we will learn about the technical path. Technical path in knowledge management can be further categorized into:

- knowledge management system development,
- knowledge management system analyst,
- knowledge management system trainer.

In this path, KM system development can be divided into:

- knowledge management Microsoft SharePoint[100] development,
- knowledge management software customization developer,
- knowledge management social operating system development,
- knowledge management individual knowledge management system and development,
- knowledge management function-based development,
- knowledge management service-based development,
- knowledge management product development,
- knowledge management product test services development.

The other paths are closely aligned to all the above subprogram paths.

FACILITATION KNOWLEDGE MANAGEMENT PATH

Facilitation is the core job path, where facilitation is to:

- Engage with the leadership, engage with the management team, engage with the grassroot-level knowledge worker. This is the core job to understand the priorities, business challenges, and develop the requirements.

- Engage various stakeholders between various entities to further the conversation, to create new knowledge until the existing problems are understood. Jot down the future path.

- Engage knowledge workers to understand their needs and provide a platform to develop and design their own knowledge management.

- Develop Taxonomy for the enterprise, functions or any organizational entity.

- Develop Use Case for primary and secondary audience knowledge gaps based on assessments and audits.

- Engage with the organization entities for peer-to-peer learning; mentor, mentee relationship enhancement; contextual and organization development[101].

- Work with various functions to receive inputs and coordinating with the technology team to come out with knowledge management solutions.

- The community of practices moderation, Shepard complete lifecycle of CoP (Close of Play).

CONTENT - KNOWLEDGE MANAGEMENT PATH

Content in itself is quite a wide area of paths with an amalgamation of print and media fields. In this path, content development, content creation and content management are the core ingredients of the job.

This path includes creating the content for:

- articles,

- write up stories,

- success stories,

- case studies,

- IP (Intellectual Property) drafting,

- authoring, etc.

The level of expertise for content is already on par with the media and publishing industry.

Example: graphic creation icons, new logos, KM logo, etc. are all path of the content which we are referring to here.

It's not necessary that you need to have this competency.

These competency resources could be based on shared services or outsourced to the gig market. Get things done based on the budgetary constraints or knowledge of the organization. Define the content knowledge management rules in this path.

KM SUPPORT PATH

The need for the KM support path surfaces when the systems are defined, and implemented. Every KM system needs support contact with the user who he could reach out to and share the challenges, issues, new requirements, etc.

The KM support needs to provide complete guidance and assistance to the user group. The success of the KM function depends entirely on this front line. The user has to be sensitive, cooperative and technical in business concepts. The user needs to go the extra mile to satisfy the customer and business needs with holistic support and empathy.

Important note:

At the end of the day, it is the business user who needs maximum support to complete or do the day-to-day activity on operations and tasks seamlessly. It is the user who has to create results for the organization. Therefore, there is the underlying support, which the knowledge management team will have to provide or cater to the user.

It could be providing support in creating or facilitating workshops, collaboration sites, providing technical assistance related to content updates in the KM portal and so on.

PROGRAM MANAGEMENT PATH OR LEADERSHIP KNOWLEDGE MANAGEMENT PATH

In large MNCs, big corporates KMs sometimes are decentralized. However, whether it is centralized or decentralized, KM governance is essential which has also been mentioned in Chapter 10: Knowledge Enablers (under the Governance section). The KM program office has to develop the overall portfolios, project's and KM initiatives as and when required. These should be developed based on the breadth and width of KM penetration.

- The individual has to play a leadership role, get commitments from management, get budgets allocated, get resources available to the overall KM strategy.

- The individual needs to understand the complete life cycle of knowledge management, implementation of the small, medium, and large scale systems, programs, and initiatives.

- The individual should have a comprehensive understanding of technology, infrastructure, phases of implementation.

- The organization needs to empower business leaders, identify high potential knowledge management individuals at all levels.

- Create the structure for knowledge management catalyst, identify individuals with champion roles, understand trends, technology practices in the market, seek opportunities again as a business of priorities.

- Manage overall reporting system, governance, reviews, meetings, updates, success meets, a weekly call, et cetera.

- Participate in thought leadership and answer experience of knowledge commitment, world culture in organizing external supplier organization, government, et cetera.

- Need to have a reasonably strategical managing reporting, flare for experimentation and translate the organization's needs, flexible, practical, agile execution-oriented, pragmatic, good observer, listener, leadership delegation, good delegator of KM management duties.

- Manage resources, manage finance and manage lead teams virtually and at physical locations.

- Showcase the outcomes, effectiveness of KM concepts, theories and presentations to the management.

To be able to dirty one's own hand, get to the ground and make things happen, facilitate leadership forum, envisioning forum.

RESEARCH AND INNOVATION KM PATH

These are the multiple roles of specialization to understand the new technologies, solutions, challenges, which are engulfing the organization and come out with a solution concerning technology practices, emerging practices, emerging technologies in the field of knowledge management.

Hence, the research path is essential in terms of devising and developing practices, tools, system methodology, and frameworks in the organization while working along with the business function.

CHANGE MANAGEMENT/COMMUNICATION PATH

In this path, the knowledge management team needs to perform the following roles:

- Design various engagement methods
- Newsletter, planned roadshows
- Communication across corporate
- Needs to run conferences, KM seminars, knowledge sharing sessions
- Managing events, manage various activities, events, external events, internal events, workshops with customers, with vendors, suppliers
- Communicate with communities externally
- Needs to manage the interface with the external organization

- Needs to design campaigns, introduce posters, coordinate with speakers, manage schedules and workshop presentations, etc.

EXPERIENCES REQUIRED FOR KM ROLES

Overall KM management competency could be charted down in terms of leadership and program management. A minimum requirement is from 12 years to 30 years of experience:

- Facilitation path: 6 to 30 years of experience.
- Content path: at least 2 to 30 years of experience, 2 to 12 years of experience.
- Technology path: 2 to 10 years, 15 years of experience.
- Support: 0 to 2 years of experience.
- Research path innovation: 0 to 30 years of experience.

Ideally, these paths and work experience provide a view of how to select the competent profile in each of these roles. There's probably certain classification or junior roles with whose experience they can become mentors. And after working with various organizations, you become competent in those areas.

These paths and streams of work related to KM can be performed by multiple personal or one or two people, this entirely depends on the organization's expandability.

Competency and competency management are two different things in KM. Competency for KM roles and in KM functions are different from organizational competency management.

Can I play competency management for KM functions too?

For that, a KM function needs to get established across the business and corporate house. Even though, the finance function is a critical function; I envision the knowledge management department to be more critical to manage the unprecedented amount of knowledge, and remote working; the new form of work culture that the pandemic has bestowed on the globe.

AWARENESS AND COMMUNICATION

Knowledge management programs and initiatives work differently for different organizations. There are separate corporate communication teams that communicate a lot on the organizational update, news, HR updates, policies, etc. However, when we are talking about communication in terms of knowledge management, the fundamental requirement for KM is awareness.

Communication and awareness are two faces of the same coin or they both can be mentioned as a cause and effect. Communication[102] and awareness are the same as cause and effect.

The KM team or the KMS team needs to communicate with its audience not only after the KM system launch, but also needs to adopt a robust and systematic communication system approach. It needs to be well-planned which has already been discussed in Chapter 7: Planning.

Here is a brief idea of the knowledge management communication framework.

The knowledge management communication framework could have:

- Multiple communication channels like emails, display boards, newsletters, posters, updates, etc.
- You can use multiple communication languages, your local language, English, etc.
- Communication mediums could use the print medium, digital medium and paper medium.

Then you could also have a one-to-one, one-to-many, focused target-based audience. You can have push communication or you can set up a special group to have pull communication.

You could also have communication based on the timelines of the project like start to end, giving out information based on various phases or the lifecycles or the milestones or any frequent updates.

Communication could also include gatherings, meetings, training, roadshows.

Personal communications are important in terms of individual target communication, group target communication, audience-targeted communication.

Communication could also be only internal to the organization, external to the organization, client communication, employee-based communication, process-centric communication, business-centric communication or vendor-specific communications.

Communication could take place at various mediums in terms of the conversation between people or virtual, physical or group or social gatherings

This encompasses the entire KM communication framework; designing communication for each strategy, planning features, advantages, scheme of KMS needs to be integrated.

Over-communication might also not work in KM, as people might start ignoring too much email communication as well.

Therefore, it is very important to plan such communication on email which is really critical and that adds value to the employee's work, project or learning. Utilize your poster charts to make the communication more appealing. Use infographics data, animation, knowledge management maps, etc. in the communication medium to make it more visual.

As you engage with the users, leaders, clients, customers through communication on KM and its application, process advantage, behaviors and positive results, the users will be able to see the results produced through KMS, and will provide a unique opportunity to a knit, open and transparent environment.

Increasing participation, increasing mutual trust and respect for experts will contribute to other development, learning and act as a catalyst for important business outcomes.

This kind of communication has a multifold effect:

- It provides better awareness about the knowledge management system within and across our corporate audience.

- It binds together the organization and entity, thereby learning various ways to create success.

- It provides a bonding across the organization that engages people and leadership vision is being aligned and taken together.

- It helps the organization self-realize its true potential.

DOCUMENTED INFORMATION

This is a very important aspect as the entire knowledge management system needs to be documented for all the clauses requirements. All the documents, action items, MoMs (Minutes of Meeting), action tracking, meeting reviews, project reviews, outcomes and action-taken need to be documented efficiently[103].

The general rule of ISO 9001 QMS (Quality Management System) documentation applies to ISO 30401 KMS standard as well when it comes to document control, creation, modification and updation, along with the access control. For example, the KM planning document could have the control history of the versions, a modification-approved contributor to that document.

You could also have one more set, which could be a level of document talking about the accessibility in terms of the confidentiality level of that document and how it can be controlled, whether is it open to all, is it open only to the organization? Further, you can also determine if the document can be made public or restricted within the organization or it is highly confidential, neither shareable nor confidential, but restricted within the organization to certain parties. Then the document control needs to be adopted from the original information; quality management policies and information security policies must be framed.

These are the factors that are applicable when it comes to document management.

There are various document tracking systems that need to be adopted to make sure the policies are available easily to any employee in the organization.

Procedures of knowledge management, SOPs (Standard Operating Procedure) and guidelines should be available with all the versions, history and approval, registers, review, all the information should be available.

At the same time, the next level of the KM plan, strategy, operation plans reviewed and approved by the top management are required.

Then there are templates, guides, best practices, toolkits and various other aspects for general use, which again should be available in the correct version history and need to be controlled.

Then the next set of documents are the ones related to reports, governance, reporting structure, review notes, dashboards, action notes, action tracker, risk meeting, projects risk analysis, opportunity analysis, knowledge management requirements, document management requirements, record management requirements and documentation on each of these systems must be available.

These should be accessible not only to the knowledge management system, but also to the appropriate audience and the users of these systems. Wherever confidentiality, highly-confidential or classified information needs to be restricted, it has to be restricted according to the information security policy.

The documents which are generated need to have an expiration date and it is necessary to set an expiration timeline for a document, for example, there are policies that certain organizations have as per the Sarbanes-Oxley Act[104]. The average record management[105] is generally seven years of documentation after which, re-documentation has to be done. The organizations located in various countries and various states depend on what is the state law and land law which determine the documentation, retrieval and archival process. This needs to be strictly adhered to for the contents.

The contents in the KMS system should also have this archival expiry date which can be renewed based on the requirement. The document layer and control have multiple aspects in terms of the moderation forum. It could be in the community of practices, the communities of interest, public portal contents, RACI matrix.

These are the various contents that need to be managed, reviewed, archived and deleted based on the validity of it and what is the policy on those things also needs to be documented.

- Who are the users?
- What are their rights?
- What are the access controls that need to be documented?

Digital documentation in terms of the knowledge management function documentation, outlook, strategies, records, reviews, decisions needs to be maintained. The portal pages of various knowledge management content or dashboard-related knowledge management reports; all need to be documented.

Physical documentation, whether it's manual, receipts, records, posters; all needs to be documented or available as evidence in a physical or digital format.

Portal content management, contents in the various documents, contents in the pages, contents in the links; all should be updated, need to be current and working. If the content of the links is not working, then the content needs to be replaced or the links have to be removed.

When it comes to the governance of that documentation, the RACI matrix, the guidelines, master document, etc. all need to be managed and updated.

These are the different layers of documentation, which need to be taken care of from the knowledge management's perspective. Of course, at the highest level, each of these processes needs to be listed and the requirement should be mapped to this document so that it's easier for the new member to understand the entire KM function processes, services, supports, products, systems, etc. Also, it will ease showcasing evidence by the auditee i.e. to showcase the documentation to the auditor during the audition.

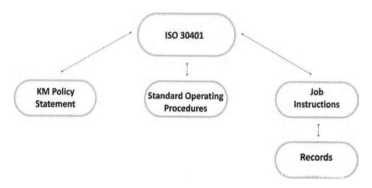

Diagram I.K.D.T.1 - ISO KM Documentation Tree (Example)

Diagram I.K.D.L-2 - ISO KM Documentation Layers

CONTENT OF PROCEDURES

A procedure must have the following contents to be a full-fledged procedure:

- General Description of the activity with objective and aims

- Details of input and expected outputs of that particular activity

- Details of the title of the individual or individuals responsible for that activity

- List of standards or reference to the standards that list the resources needed to perform the activity

- Quality standards of the input and output along with control measures and methodology used to measures. Details of limit samples

- Documentary requirements for performing the activity. (Customer-Centric KM[106], Product-Centric KM, etc.)

- Reference to specific work instructions related to these procedures including the business impacts

- The details on benchmarking the quality and effectiveness of KM activity

- Details on instructions pertaining to activity along with remarks on KMS for the procedures

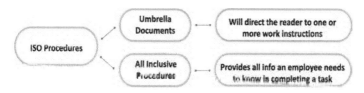

Diagram I.K.P.D.T - ISO KM procedures documentation Type

ISO 30401 KM PROCEDURES - TYPES

Listing of KM records:

- Information on applicable Information Management Security, laws and regulations

- Complaint records

- Training records including the verification of effectiveness

- Process information including impact identification

- KM system information

- Inspection, maintenance and support records

- Information about all the interested parties

- Information about the security and archival policies

- Records indicating how KM aspects were identified and reviewed
- Follow up on corrective actions
- Management review records including evaluation of technological options and considerations of KM aspects when planning the expansion

The above provides a few examples in terms of documentation upon which the organization needs to build what is deemed to be appropriate. Documentation in itself should not create barriers during the execution of KM activities and deliverables.

CHAPTER TWELVE
OPERATIONS

KM Operations, like any function, are a multitude of operational and transactional activities, duties, tasks and milestones, with regard to managing KM system technologies, support users, training the users on the system, providing various support in terms of knowledge orchestration and other KM services. These services could be facilitation services, provide content, content management and content development services, provide content purging and archive services, provide process updates to fulfill an event, meeting business requirements.

The key to drive knowledge management operations is to provide continuous support to business users towards their function department, activities and knowledge orchestration or higher-order KM requirements. These are further divided in terms of knowledge services and operations.

The management operation varies from the following matrixes:

- Knowledge management stand-alone
- KM function-driven/ group-driven

- Knowledge management services
- Knowledge management services at the enterprise level

For every category of knowledge management establishment in our organization, KM's implementation and support process need to be defined. This can be done by the individual performing various roles or we can develop a group of personnel to play various KM roles depending on the category of the knowledge management system and the organization it dwells in.

At the beginning of the KM program or initiative, the company wants to use minimal resources to make sure it works in the first place and then expand the team. As long as the users are being supported to catering to their mentioned knowledge needs, it's imperative for the KM function and team to expedite and support the audience.

WHAT IS KM SUPPORT?

It varies from industry to industry. In the last century, there were curators/experts for art museums/libraries where they exactly knew about the museum display or books to read the recommendation on various subjects. Similarly, here are two KM curated questions or support services examples for *Project-Based services*.

- May I know whether we have done similar projects?
- What are the challenges in this particular area, topic?

Product-based KM

- I need to know how to fix the error or need to correct the issue, et cetera.

- How to KM: I need this methodology to apply for oil and gas?

- How do I go about what are the process areas? What are their taxonomies?

- What are their business areas... sub-business areas and emerging problems?

This would help us define the problem and development. We can also design the Product-based KM[107] solution roadmap based on such questions.

Client-Facing KM

- I need to submit this document to RFP (Request for Proposal), have we done similar work?

- Can't I reuse them for past and responses?

These are some of the examples based on how curated knowledge services could be developed in the organization.

Now, let me walk you through standardization in terms of knowledge management, standalone systems where the support is more in terms of getting content to the users. Marketing team to document the records of the Client's query and support KM systems by sharing reusable contents, templates, etc. The scope is limited and happens at the local level. Any system needs some kind of support, it could be content-related, knowledge-related, or lessons/learning-related, et cetera in case of a standalone.

At the same time, it can be broadened up into multiple parts for organizations.

Knowledge management service could branch out into:

- knowledge management consulting

- knowledge management workshops
- knowledge management facilitation
- knowledge management systems like service collaborative spaces, photo services, knowledge services
- taxonomy development services
- KM repository that requires document management is a system that recommends the core management system
- KM product development
- new R&D areas
- KM practices development
- KM framework developments, technology and services

These are some of the supporting services which the KM function can impart, which would greatly add value to the organization.

Now, let's learn about the KM support framework. There are 7 layers in the KM support framework.

The first layer is the digital KM services. It could be in terms of webinars, web collaboration services, e-learning modules, document management spaces, records management portals or content management intranets. These are some of the services which could be provided to the organization.

Physical - Setting up conferences, workshops on conferences, knowledge camps, knowledge jams, knowledge café, knowledge fair; all these may need infrastructure as well as a supporting structure. However, conducting such kinds of workshops is important.

Then comes content; content in terms of document links, materials, artifacts, websites, weblinks, apps, app links, member library, membership, external knowledge membership, knowledge repository, knowledge database, lessons learned database, the content generation and updation into this content aspect could also be one of the important content management aspects.

Strategic support in terms of defining strategic missions, vision roadmap of the knowledge management development, solution strategy of the organization based on the classical framework, our idea-oriented or technology-oriented solutioning, our tactical solutioning, how we are going about achieving it, who's our target audience.

Some more questions that must be considered are how are you going to engage with the audience? What is the engagement timeline? What are the methods you are going to use? Would all be included in the tactical solutioning?

There are times when you need to support a certain department in developing their specific requirements as a standalone, as they know exactly what they need.

There could also be times when you need to define a strategic level at the highest level so that it could get to the lowest of the requirements and customizable to any department, service line, business lines, business units, product lines, research units, manufacturing units.

The fifth layer is operational. Operational is about providing day-to-day activity support. Where do I find this document? Where do I find this lesson? In terms of references, follow SLAs and conditions, dashboard reports, performance management, TAT turnaround times.

Basically, it has to do with what are the various activities, whether it is developing portals, or developing core taxonomy, whether it is designing taxonomy. These are going to become parts of the operational tasks.

The seventh is practices. In the practices, the support and knowledge management frameworks are about developing frameworks for the organization. From the knowledge management's perspective, it may include developing tool kits, templates, guides, how to use the body of knowledge, case study, not only limited to knowledge management function. It could be done as a consulting service to our departments of marketing and sales, research and innovation organizations, any business function, any departments, et cetera.

The systems they support are about knowledge management. If there are multiple program management systems, there could be a lot of areas like knowledge management process, development systems, KM system, communication systems and content management systems. All of these need to be defined, controlled, measured and monitored so that the entire KM function works smoothly and is aligned to the original knowledge management's mission and vision. It follows a certain plan and it chooses its milestone, creating results on the ground, being effective and yielding results with the business operations.

In an earlier topic, we discussed about KMs standalone, operations support to knowledge management system or the regional level knowledge management system at the enterprise level, knowledge management system at the function level. The support and services required for each of these are focused on the scope of the knowledge management area that varies from organization to organization based on these four broad themes. If the KM is enterprise-driven, it covers huge multiple areas, which we will discuss in the next chapter.

When the KM is functional-driven, it, again, is an enterprise-driven focus area regarding how you provide support and services in terms of knowledge management. When it comes to knowledge management standalone support and services, it is very specific to a certain organization's smaller area or it can be individual-driven or a specific role-driven knowledge management system. However, it also needs support and services which must be scheduled for the primary and secondary audiences.

CHAPTER THIRTEEN

PERFORMANCE EVALUATION

MONITORING MEASUREMENT ANALYSIS AND EVALUATION

Monitoring the KM system, KM programs, KM projects at every step is essential. All the stages are critical.

The key to a successful KM project is defining every aspect of the task, activities, milestones, and monitoring to make sure they are completed, achieved, and realized within the planned schedules.

KM measurement is a mandatory exercise for the management's continuous support for KM. As they say, what you measure, you can manage and what you manage, so can you measure. To add further to this phrase… "What you measure, you can manage in the physical and digital domain. However, when it comes to the knowledge field, human potential, intellectual capitalism and social capitalism, it is complicated."

I believe, in the KM field, it's important to measure the journey, to understand the length traveled in KM life cycles.

One's knowledge thought can change the world. One man can change the course of history and can become de facto for new development or destruction. In the same context, the measurement scale for KM needs to be established. Understanding the nature of humans, understanding the nature of social operating dynamics, understanding the nature of business priorities and requirements are essential. Knowledge organization or knowledge entities need to develop certain ways to measure the knowledge flows, knowledge conception, knowledge reuse, knowledge storage and knowledge applications.

Based on this context, I could talk about the knowledge management measurement pre-assessment scale. How to develop a measurement scale?

You could look at knowledge flows in the digital medium, in the conversations in the world; social world, the relatedness world and all the relationship world.

Again, in this conversation world, we can look at the physical domain, where all the conversations are happening physically.

Is it happening through meetings? Is it happening in terms of workshops? Is it happening one-to-one? Is it that happening between a group of people?

You need to identify where are these conversations happening, whether on the phone, on email or in face-to-face conversations.

If it is electronics, you can also look from the electronic perspective, whether it's mobile electronics or gadgets in terms of digital, whether it's happening on the forum, whether it is happening through our document sharing, whether it is on the work's collaboration spaces or in the augmented reality.

A similar pattern also applies to the social world. The social world is a group of people talking in a physical space or a group of people talking in a digital forum or group of people coming together in augmented reality or virtual reality.

In the relationship-based world, it is about the culture of how people are being mentored, coached or trained. For example, in the case of learning how to swim, the person needs to be with the mentee and learn on the floor (here water).

Most of the conversations one-to-one, one-to-many, many-to-many are all happening on the digital medium and in future-augmented reality. This is one pointer to underline the essence of knowledge flows. Similarly, it is important to map the points of knowledge assets generation, dissemination and consumption; These are some examples of how one can start seeing the patterns and real-world transactions to come up with the measurement definitions and metrics.

Measurement of KM has always been a topic of greatest challenge and debate area, however, the below five elements provide a context in which KM could be measured. Is the measurement of KM absolute? No, it can never be, and it will never happen. In the context of business, the scoping Knowledge problem does help us in defining the KM measurements by using these elements.

Based on these domains and dimensions, we can identify a few key elements of measurements, they are:

- Measurement of Engagement – What is the kind of engagement a KM Program/System is able to generate

- Measurement of Effectiveness- How effective is the KMS to the user, or what value is the KM creating for the user

- Measurement of Collaboration- How are people collaborating among each other, what results are they producing

- Measurement of Knowledge Experience- How does one experience the ease of knowledge access and visibility around and also have access to it

- Measurement of Knowledge Innovation – How the Organizations are managing knowledge to create an innovation culture

MEASUREMENT OF ENGAGEMENT

Measurement of Engagement[108] - number of lessons learned workshops conducted, number of peer-to-peer sessions conducted, number of knowledge assets downloaded, number of discussions around a topic, number of knowledge artifacts contributed to the system, number of communications, engagement on-site- training, awareness, etc. This way, the KM team can manage to report the actual activities across various transactions between people-to-people, people-to-content, etc. You can keep adding the knowledge order needs into managing the engagements externally, customers, clients, products, etc.

For the analysis of KM operations, metrics can easily be made available with the system reporting, system logs. Physical-metrics-capture-form should be created by clocking every KM activity which occurs across the organization and represents a report. It's more often manual in nature to capture the collaboration index. It could be based on people reporting feedbacks. It is always recommended to capture the inputs of the teams and KM champions.

MEASUREMENT OF EFFECTIVENESS

Measurement of Effectiveness - The next big question that arises is, what value has been created out of the workshop facilitation? Did the reusable artifact help somebody cut down their time? These could be effective elements in the KM. Most of the challenges of measurement surface in this area.

We can look at various attributes in terms of document portal access. These could be the number of visitors visiting the portal, the number of documents or blogs being accessed or blogs being written with effectiveness. We can also know about:

- How many people have reused this document?
- What is the effectiveness of these reuse artifacts, the body of knowledge?
- Is it creating new value? If it is, how has it helped in collaboration?
- How did the project lesson help the organization to save costs in multiple projects?
- How effective is the CoPs[109]?

To capture experiential outcomes, this is the toughest and most important self-aspect. The total value created on the business is a business impact. A writer, budget, cost-saving, et cetera are more of qualitative in nature.

The form could include simple statements like 'these lessons have helped in curtailing the communication interface challenges with the window' or 'a document template saved 60 minutes of my time', et cetera. This again is related to digital matrices in terms of engagement and document contribution, documentary use lessons contribution, document creation, forum-questions posted, questions answered, Knowledge management articles and Knowledge management newsletters, success stories published, metrics report, etc.

It would be a de-function level in terms of how many numbers of reuses have been declared?

How many case studies have been published?

How many knowledge sharing sessions have been conducted at various functions level?

MEASUREMENT OF COLLABORATION

Measurement of Collaboration[110] is based on the soft value being generated as new learning out of sharing within each other, between the group of people, what outcomes or what knowledge bodies are being created for the organizations? It is an offshoot of effectiveness, however there could be stress on the social dimension. It is a unique space that once created, in the collaborative conversation, we can read the soft value that could ignite new ideas and new insights that could have an exponential index.

And that would provide a second order of collaboration value. In an experiential world, it would provide an organization with a boost in terms of enhancement, focus on share-ability and knowledge can be exchanged freely. It stems from the organizational culture, how the leaders project their vision, how they participate, and how they exhume behaviors of inclusion, participation, open and transparent environment are the pre-essentials.

Now coming to augmented reality or virtual reality, we are looking at the program argumentation reality, again, engagement, effectiveness, the collaborative index would become the norm of the day going forward. It is essential to assess soft aspects of organizational structure and the measurement scale could be created

These three become the foundational elements of measurements. To make an evaluation based on this, the KM management function could come up with the KM dashboard. It is important to understand that knowledge is not just about numbers.

If I say one, two, three, four, five... these are just numerals, but employee 1, employee 2, employee 3, employee 4 are not the same. This distinction is very important in the field of knowledge and innovation.

People cannot be quantified just as numbers. The quality of experts, senior experts, business leaders are not just numbers. So it is important for the organization's KM programs to be effective and contribute to the organization's development.

The concept of driving KM based on Statistics is anti-KM from my experience. If you truly want to nurture a collaborative mindset and the organization needs to have a holistic vision, it is important to understand that the metrics are important. However, it's not very important from the point of view of the organization's development; creating value is paramount.

The KM should work to prepare the organization for uncertainties, face the future bravely, and get in the mode of preparedness. Numbers are not the supreme need for the organization, but these are an essential part of the requirements as an indicator. The KM evaluation can be done on KM values which could be a greater area to develop.

The organization needs to have a structure to manage this review analysis process. If knowledge management is a stand-alone KMS, it could be of a local level. Certainly, the review process in terms of finances is a basic requirement. But if it is driven at the enterprise-level, whether it is at the business function level, regional level, enterprise-level, state-level or national-level, it is always important to have a structure in terms of looking at various KM activities happening every week, achievements every month, communications every fortnight or milestones achieved every six months. Delegate such events every year and realign the knowledge management plan every two years at least.

A support structure in terms of who is going to produce reports is another level of the structure. This needs to be created so that the various reports are generated by the owner of the report. Certain questions should be reviewed, like:

- Who's the owner of this report?

- Who's going to review the report and what are the actions to be taken after reviewing this action report?

- At what frequency should these reports be generated?

There are some of the structures which are going to help the organization. Again, knowledge management needs to define the KM's KPIs (Key Performance Indicators), manage and measure them. However, the corporate world comes under the radar of challenges in the absence of KPIs as part of standard requirements. hence the KPIs are there for the teams, they need to evaluate based on the organizational KM KPIs, functional KM KPIs and role-based KM KPIs.

Similarly, these should be structured from service KPIs to individual KPIs and product KPIs to individual KPIs. And again, at the individual level, it could be based on contribution, reuse and mentoring at the service level. It could be the frameworks, products, etc., and a KPA individual could have a number of ideas, innovation, etc.

This could become a part of their appraisal process. Again, there are certain metrics reports, which need to be generated over a period of time.

The KM function should take the onus of managing the KM, KPIs dashboard every month and yearly. The KM function should review the progress of KPIs achieved with the management every year just like any other strategic management area.

These are some of the examples in terms of deriving various structures.

And it is very important to fathom that just metrics in themselves are not very important, however, these should provide the navigation and big picture to the overall knowledge management program.

At the same time, these metrics also help the leadership team in understanding the context, engagement and effectiveness of the programs they are sponsoring. It also helps the organizations to understand the gaps and challenges.

MEASUREMENT OF KNOWLEDGE EXPERIENCE

Measurement of Knowledge Experience is an important element. At the end of the day what counts is how one role experiences empowerment in the organization with one's learning and development of competency. One empowered with knowledge infrastructure whether in Digital, Physical, Social domains, getting fulfillment individually and at the workplace are altogether new ways of measuring Knowledge experience, which should be explored and developed further.

MEASUREMENT OF KNOWLEDGE INNOVATION

Measurement of Knowledge Innovation[111] – End of the day, you might have great KM engagement, collaboration, effectiveness; however, if the organization is going to become bankrupt; then the whole process of KM measurement is meaningless. Similarly, if all the organizations are successful and the division in the society increases – digital divide, literacy divide, have's and have not's; end of the day, how KM can promote sustainable innovation to promote social harmony, co-operation, and well-being of societies are the greatest contributions to nations and world peace.

Once the organization can crack these 5 elemental measurements, it will require impetus and also insights from the leadership and management team to design effective strategies in terms of knowledge management. These are the strategies where there's business management, business strategy, marketing strategy. Most of the knowledge management systems could drive some of the strategies, redesign and provide feedback loop within the business.

MANAGEMENT REVIEW

In the performance evaluation, we have already talked about the review's reporting structure. Some of the aspects of operations are day-to-day activities, measurement, monthly metrics, qualitative measurement, fortnightly key highlights and success story measurement systems are reported in the dashboard along with milestones as human measurement.

Internal audit, external audit and management review are as important as having effective knowledge management systems. As long as the knowledge management systems are effective, the internal processes can be documented. Users in the organization or employees in the organization know their role in this indirect knowledge management system, their contribution and the usage of the knowledge management system. And there's a culture between and across the organization where sharing happens naturally and the matrices are developed based on the organization's requirement. The knowledge management systems are developed based on scoped stakeholder's requirements. These tools work well. There should be a team supporting the operations and day-to-day activities. For the period of monitoring, every aspect of the activities and whether they are all aligned with the scope are very important.

KM AUDITS

There are millions of organizations across the globe, who do not have KM as a focused area, they should start buying ISO KMS standard and move up in the KM cycle by organizing their knowledge effectively. If the organization already has a KM system in the organization, they can use the KM standards requirement to map the gaps and fulfill them. Once done, the organization can self-declare itself as ISO 30401 KMS standard compliant. To receive external certification, the organization needs to prepare for the complete audit and initiate the Certification process.

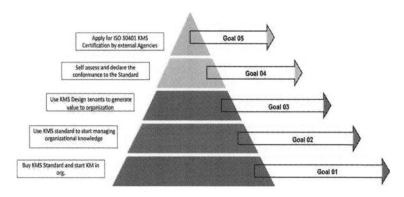

Diagram K.M.G.A.S – KMS Global Adaptability Steps

In this section, we are going to overview the certification process. KMS audit is a systematic and documentation verification process where an organization's conformance on the following requirements of ISO 30401 standard is followed. The audit merely certifies whether the organization has been able to implement the standard requirements as prescribed and is free of non-conformances to the standard.

Audits are important to align and get that third body perspective of the KM areas, which are important to the organization. Unlike quality audits, a knowledge management audit needs to work at different levels and needs to look at the organization in a different dimension.

The audits are not simply to check the documentation, these must measure the effectiveness of the knowledge management system, how they are creating the sharing culture. How they are impacting the business outcome using KMS is the most important aspect of the auditing criteria.

In these audits, Gemba walks, walk the floor, meet and speak to people at different levels and understanding the effectiveness of the knowledge management system will be determined. Some of the questions in context to internal auditing or the auditing, in general, are as follows:

- What to look at from the KM scope?
- How KMS is impacting?
- How are the solutions making a difference in the organization?
- How's the management supporting the KM initiative?
- What are the effects of knowledge sharing in the organization?
- How is the conversation flowing in the organization, is it engaging, encouraging to learn from mistakes, or it is a punishing culture?
- What are the multiple aspects of KM principles playing in the background?

In terms of the knowledge management program assessments, the organizations need to plan their internal and external audits and should be part of the four-five-year KM plan. Make sure that the internal audits are conducted frequently. My recommendation is to have at least two internal audits before going for external audits if you have started KM newly in the organization.

HOW ARE THE INTERNAL AUDITS CONDUCTED?

The noncompliance and the other observations need to be documented and appropriate actions should be taken during the Internal Audit. Later, while doing the external audit, you should be able to showcase the evidence of internal audiences, observations and how they are being handled or resolved.

The Internal audit plan has certain important steps:

1. The initial Internal audit kickoff plan: ensure complete documentation, updation and structuring are complete.

2. Then the internal auditor is nominated either outside of the company or outside of the KM team, we need a third-party to do the KM Internal Audit.

3. Once the auditor is confirmed, set up a meeting to discuss the business and the scope of the audit. It is important that the auditor should be familiar with the ISO-30401 or the standard.

4. When these are agreed upon, then on the day of internal audits, kick off the audit. Go through the entire documentation and requirements based on standards.

5. The auditor reviews the necessary clauses against the documents/evidence/responses and collects or

documents it. Based on the template, it is always advisable to put on or map the entire documentation including the name and particular requirements of the clauses.

6. As the auditor collects the entire evidence, he goes back to review each of the clauses and the requirements to ascertain if complete and then provides an internal audit report.

7. And the next phase of the preparation of the audit report can be sparked off.

In this report phase, the internal auditor can prepare all the observations, insist on what's good or what has been observed:

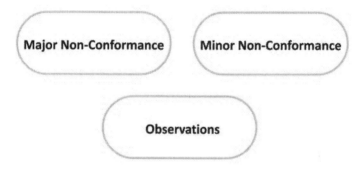

Diagram I.K.A.R.C- ISO KM Audit Report categories

1. Major Non-Conformance – If a major clause is not implemented.

2. Minor Non-Conformance- If the evidence is available in parts and not complete or partial gaps in requirements.

3. Observation – Observations are Auditor's overall KMS system review comments like what went well, what

were the good practices, what could be improved, etc. It does not necessarily mean something is missing.

The internal audit report should be prepared and shared with the Internal Audit preparation team.

The report should be shared with the organization committee on the organization or requirement. The KM team should follow steps to close NCRs, in this way, the gap analysis of ISO clause requirements assessment is met.

This could be repeated every two years, before going for an external audit.

EXTERNAL AUDIT

If the organization requests to apply for external certification, then it should plan for an external audit.

External auditing and certification are two different steps. In this step of External Auditing, an accredited ISO auditor is invited to assess the organizational KM and provide the report based on his assessment, the company, if complies, can declare itself as ISO compliant.

If necessary, the company can apply for ISO 30401 Certification, which is the next step after external audition.

It is important for the organization to obtain permission from the management and quote the required budget to go for external auditing and certification.

CERTIFICATION OF ORGANIZATIONS

- Implementation of the management system:

  Before being audited, a management system must be in operation for some time. Usually, the minimum time required by the certification bodies is 3 months.

- Internal audit and review by top management:

  Before a management system can be certified, it must have had at least one internal audit and one management review.

- Selection of the certification body (registrar):

  Each organization can select the certification body (registrar) of its choice.

- Pre-assessment audit (optional):

  An organization can choose to perform a pre-audit to identify any possible gap between its current management system and the requirements of the standard.

ORGANIZATION GETTING ISO 30401 CERTIFIED

- Companies can become certified either as practitioners to demonstrate their commitment to the application of effective practices related to the standard or as solution providers, demonstrating their commitment to providing ISO compliant audit or development services. Any organization or division of an organization can become certified, provided it has a CEO or division-head-led strategic and systematic approach to the practice involved with the standard.

- Organization audits are conducted once every three years; i.e., they must be completed by the end of the fourth year following each audit so that not more than three full years elapse between each audit.

CHAPTER FOURTEEN

CONTINUOUS IMPROVEMENT

ISO 30401 standard documentation varies from organization to organization, and relatively new to provide a common framework on the standard documentation. However, as you follow the systematic way of doing things, keep documenting the entire journey, its activities, its actions, minutes, document control, manual, policies, procedures, KPIs, dashboard, training and other activities. Documentation would go a long way to self-declare that the organization is ISO 30401 compliant.

As you build the KMS platform based on the stakeholder's requirements, there will be multiple requirements coming your way. These requirements need to be captured into the feedback system and use appropriately to develop KM services, enhancement of systems, betterment of processes embedding of KM processes, further enhancement of the systems, practices, processes, contents, etc.

When it comes to managing the feedback from management, primary audience and listening to the demand of the organization's need, the KM strategy will have to be reinvented and reenergized.

What knowledge is and the needs that are relevant today may not be relevant tomorrow with changing and shifting due to the global dynamics and pandemic.

It is essential to understand that managing one's knowledge and redirecting one's own path is very critical. It can be bolstered if the organization is managing knowledge well. However, this can be an important tenant of the organizational resilience because of which the organization can run out of business.

There are various levels of CI (Continuous Improvement) pertaining to-

1. KM strategy
2. KM operational excellence
3. KM systems architecture and Knowledge Experience
4. KM processes
5. KM content
6. KM interfaces
7. KM projects and program
8. KM governance
9. KM culture and change management
10. Organizational development and emerging technologies

CONCLUSION

We have seen how Knowledge Management System Design based on KMS standards can be applied. This book provides advanced knowledge along with sheet anchoring in terms of the knowledge field and understanding human evolution in knowledge societies.

The management studies have tried to categorize knowledge management and define it but we will not be able to define it. Why? As we consider time and space, so is Knowledge; hence we will never be able to define Knowledge management, as it falls in the Infinite series. However, definitely, only in a specific context, we have seen how knowledge needs differ in an organization, Federal Structure, government, leadership roles, etc. We can only develop knowledge circles catering to the roles in a specific context, based on the knowledge Needs order.

Once these are mapped, there are numerous classic KM Methods and IT system solutions that can be used to establish the KM system in the organization. And again the KM methods and IT systems are not the key tenants to make KM successful. The KMS can flourish when an environment is created to nurture the natural flow of sharing and receiving beyond individualistic appraisal measurement scales; developing process tenants which are part of everyday work, rather than the extra burden of work or activities; along with aiding natural way of knowledge visibility, removing all barriers which barricades one's perception of needed knowledge; imbibing a culture to take-up knowledge leadership role to fulfill one's or team's knowledge needs.

Using measurement as an enabler rather than target-oriented sales; the KM function should complement every knowledge entity it works for. It should support in the knowledge needs and fulfill them by using the best of technology. The KM function must be applied even if it is as simple as using paper and pencil or to the extent of developing AI centered work environment.

The success of organizations, societies, government agencies lies in acknowledging the challenges as they are. It lies in learning to fill the gaps to transform and contribute to developing the nations into knowledge societies.

It doesn't mean, if you are not having a KM function, you are not doing KM. KM is an integral part of how the human brain thinks, it's in everything that we do; it percolates through every function, system, process, field, past, present and future using various labels, names and categories.

As long as the organization brings all these efforts together consciously and looks at it as essential and critical; the outcome incurred over a period of time can either sustain and create great results for decades, or it could be a lost opportunity when an organization fails to manage knowledge consciously.

Knowledge management need not be an elaborate technology and high-cost rollouts. It could be simply defining folder structure and contents in each folder among the team; and making sure those are up to date; it could be a standup meeting every day- sharing the winnings and challenges in their work; it could be holding meetings between two different projects coming together to ask and get answers; it could be simply using the paper system to documenting key learnings and reading out loud to the teams. It could be mentoring new members, coaching, guiding from experts to novices is also a culture; a leader talking about his winning experience in the organization in the town hall, sharing his challenges and welcoming contribution are also knowledge culture-building exercises. Motivating knowledge workers to maintain a razor-sharp focus on the vision could be a compelling culture.

In ancient India, knowledge was always imparted orally in the Gurukul System, and the traditional father taught the ropes of trade to his son. The times and advancements have only changed the medium and channels; however, the fundamental knowledge flow has to happen from one generation to another. Humans have to learn lessons from the past to make our and the next generation's future safe and sustainable.

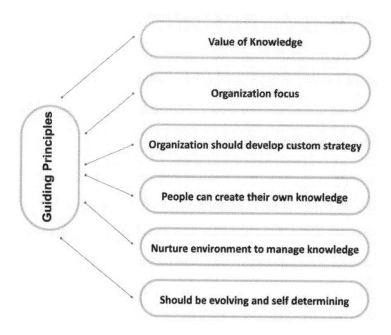

Diagram K.M.S.P – KM standard Philosophy

Knowledge Management Standard provides that same philosophy[44], it provides that school of thought which works holistically; It can be applied to any field, it can be applied to any industry, it can be applied by any individual, whichever role they play at whatever level they are in the organizations.

Like time and space, we should stop defining the meaning of KM; but should focus on Contextual KM at the center of our roles in organization, societies, government and internations.

ISO 30401 KMS standard may not be perfect in its form; however, it is complete on its merit from the contextual KM. i.e. the moment you define your KM scope, the rest of the requirements are easy to apply and create results in the organization.

End of the day, the standard in itself is a reference model for organizations to implement KMS requirements, however, it doesn't suggest how to implement KM solutions. That's where the KM functions and KM professionals can support you in developing and training the organization in the domain of Knowledge Management.

To assist the organization to implement the standard and do download useful resources, please visit http://iso30401kms.com/

KEY INSIGHTS FOR DESIGNING KMS

1. Anybody can do Knowledge Management, and it's the responsibility of every individual role and leader in the organization to manage it.

2. Leadership should foster such a culture where experts and individuals work towards developing Knowledge-

sharing and learning eco-system wherever they work.

3. KMS should work for the organization, whether getting certified for ISO 30401 or not, doesn't matter.

4. Encourage Knowledge Management at every level of the organization to enable effective knowledge flow and collaboration.

5. Technology is a key driver, keep it simple, design with the primary user.

6. KM culture is a long-term strategy, where demonstration and walk-the-talk have to happen across the hierarchy to establish a strong culture of bonding within the organization.

7. Effective KMS along with robust processes, systems, technology, people's role, outcome measurement, reviews internal and external can support in benchmarking against the ISO 30401 KMS standard.

8. Knowledge Management is not only technology, Knowledge Management is not only a culture, Knowledge Management is not only content, Knowledge Management is not only the responsibility of leadership, Knowledge Management is not only need-based; it is tapping into the consciousness of the organization and making it visible.

An organization complying with ISO 30401 KM only indicates that it has met all the clause requirements based on the standard.

1. KM Function or KM personnel in an organization is critical in every organization that could view the organization in the knowledge domain.

2. KMS can be designed for individual level, project level, business unit level, functional level, segment-level, industry-level, inter-nation level.

3. KMS is applicable to all the fields which are present today, all the fields which are emerging and all the fields which will emerge in the future.

The first step to Design KMS is to Purchase the ISO 30401 KMS standard

https://www.iso.org/standard/68683.html

Visit http://www.iso30401kms.com for more information !

BIBLIOGRAPHY

1. Knowledge Worker- https://hbr.org/2014/10/what-peter-drucker-knew-about-2020

2. Knowledge Societies- https://hbr.org/2014/10/what-peter-drucker-knew-about-2020

3. Early Human History- Stone, Bronze, and Iron Ages | Essential Humanities (essential-humanities.net); http://www.essential-humanities.net/history-overview/stone-bronze-iron-ages/

4. Industrial Revolution- Wikipedia; https://en.wikipedia.org/wiki/Industrial_Revolution

5. Knowledge Retention- Levy, M. (2011), "Knowledge retention: minimizing organizational business loss", Journal of Knowledge Management, Vol. 15 No. 4, pp. 582-600.

6. Intellectual Capital- tangibles and intangibles-a. Intellectual capital and its measurement (psu.edu); David H. Luthy; http://citeseerx.ist.psu.edu/viewdoc/download?doi=10.1.1.200.5655&rep=rep1&type=pdf; b. Sullivan, P.H. and Sullivan, P.H. (2000), "Valuing intangibles companies – An intellectual capital approach", Journal of Intellectual Capital, Vol. 1 No. 4, pp. 328-340.

7. Knowledge Management- Wikipedia | https://en.wikipedia.org/wiki/Knowledge_management

8. Allopathic- Allopathic medicine - Wikipedia; https:// en.wikipedia.org/wiki/Allopathic_medicine

9. ISO 9001- ISO 9000 - Wikipedia; https://en.wikipedia.org/ wiki/ISO_9000

10. KM technologies- Adopted from Hotaru Rei, Iso executive at Plastictecnic sdn bhd | SlideShare; https://www.slideshare. net/reihotaru90?utm_campaign=profiletracking&utm_ medium=sssite&utm_source=ssslideview

11. Knowledge-Based Economy- What is Knowledge-Based Economy | IGI Global (igi-global.com): https://www.igi-global.com/dictionary/knowledge-based-economy/16497

12. Mastering Organizational Knowledge Flow- How to make Knowledge Sharing work by Frank Leistner.

    Serenko, A., Bontis, N. and Hardie, T. (2007), "Organizational size and knowledge flow: a proposed theoretical link", Journal of Intellectual Capital, Vol. 8 No. 4, pp. 610-627

13. Types of Organizational Charts | Structure Types for Companies (creately.com) | https://creately.com/blog/ diagrams/types-of-organizational-charts/

14. Knowledge Matrix- Backstrom, Tomas & Ladan, Peter. (2002). Knowledge Matrix - a transformative organisation; https://www.researchgate.net/publication/255545168_ Knowledge_Matrix_-_a_transformative_organisation

15. Cognitive and Perceptual Constraints- 5 Perceptual and Cognitive Constraints | Learning from the Science of Cognition and Perception for Decision Making: Proceedings of a Workshop | The National Academies Press (nap.edu) | https://www.nap.edu/read/25118/chapter/6

16. Binney, D. (2001), "The knowledge management spectrum – understanding the KM landscape", Journal of Knowledge Management, Vol. 5 No. 1, pp. 33-42.

17. Knowledge Sources- Sources of Knowledge | Sources of Knowledge | Top Hat

18. Organization Life Cycles- Wikipedia

19. Information Age- Wikipedia; https://en.wikipedia.org/wiki/Information_Age

20. Colonization- Wikipedia; https://en.wikipedia.org/wiki/Colonization

21. Knowledge Work- https://www.mckinsey.com/business-functions/organization/our-insights/rethinking-knowledge-work-a-strategic-approach

22. Knowledge Economy- Drucker, Peter (1969). The Age of Discontinuity; Guidelines to Our Changing Society. New York: Harper and Row.

23. History of navigation- Wikipedia; https://en.wikipedia.org/wiki/History_of_navigation#Age_of_exploration

24. Management- Wikipedia; https://en.wikipedia.org/wiki/Management

25. Innovations- Top Innovation that changed the world ; The 10 Inventions that Changed the World (nationalgeographic.com)

26. Cycle of Individuals- Duration of working life - statistics - Statistics Explained (europa.eu)

27. Knowledge Erosion- Ahmad, Atif & Tscherning, Heidi & Bosua, Rachelle & Scheepers, Rens. (2015). Guarding Against the Erosion of Competitive Advantage: A Knowledge Leakage Mitigation Model

28. Knowledge Infrastructure- Sivan, Yesha. (2000). Nine Keys to a Knowledge Infrastructure: A Proposed Analytic Framework for Organizational Knowledge Management. 495-500

29. Knowledge Lifecycles- *Julian Birkinshaw and Tony Sheehan (2002)*, Managing the Knowledge Life Cycle (mit.edu)

30. Invention of Machines- Timeline of historic inventions - Wikipedia

31. Products Development- Industrial Revolution Inventions - Industrial Era Inventions (interestingengineering.com)

32. Indutrialization- The Industrialization of Agriculture | Encyclopedia.com

33. Experential Knowledge- https://en.wikipedia.org/wiki/ Experiential_knowledge

34. Body of Knowledge- Body of knowledge - Wikipedia

35. Knowledge Management Philosophy- Journal of Knowledge Management Practice, (tlainc.com)

36. Digital Spaces- Kalantzis Cope, Phillip. (2011). Emerging Digital Spaces in Contemporary Society: Properties of Technology.

37. Social Spaces- Council Post: Why Companies Should Incorporate Social Spaces In The Office (forbes.com) ; Lynn Metz, 2019

38. Knowledge Proximity- The Roles and Measurements of Proximity in Sustained Technology Development: A Literature Review: Inter-firm Technological Proximity and Knowledge Spillovers www.mof.go.jp › pri › pp_review › ppr13_03_05 (google.com) ; Christian Omobhude and Shih-Hsin Chen (2019)

39. KM Functions- Departmentalization - Wikipedia

40. Classical KM- Zawiła-Niedźwiecki, Janusz. (2015). Structuring Knowledge Management – Classical Theory, Strategic Initiation And Operational Knowledge Management (part I). Foundations of Management. 7. 10.1515/fman-2015-0041

41. KM System Framework- Systems development life cycle - Wikipedia

42. Knowledge Workers- https://hbr.org/2014/10/what-peter-drucker-knew-about-2020

43. Understanding Programs and Projects (pmi.org) | https://www.pmi.org/learning/library/understanding-difference-programs-versus-projects-6896

44. Functional Decomposition- an overview | ScienceDirect Topics: https://www.sciencedirect.com/topics/computer-science/functional-decomposition

45. RACI Matrix- Responsibility assignment matrix - Wikipedia

46. Business KM Requirements Documents- Ethan Raisal (1999): The McKinsey Way: Using the techniques of the world's Top strategic consultants to help you and your business

47. KM Architecture Planning Document- Chua, Alton. (2004). Knowledge management system architecture: A bridge between KM consultants and technologists. International Journal of Information Management - INT J INFORM MANAGE. 24. 87-98. 10.1016/j.ijinfomgt.2003.10.003

48. Document Sharing Workspace- Document collaboration - Wikipedia

49. Forums to Discuss- Internet forum - Wikipedia

50. KM Self-Assessment- Knowledge Sharing Tools and Methods Toolkit - KM Self Assessment (kstoolkit.org); https://kstoolkit.org/KM+Self+Assessment

51. KM Roadmap Document- Mohanraj, Prasanna. (2010). Knowledge Management – A Road Map for Winning Organization. SSRN Electronic Journal. 10.2139/ssrn.1616458.

52. KM Solution- Oliver Serrat, (2017) Knowledge Solutions-Tools, Methods, and Approaches to Drive Development Forward and Enhance Its Effects

53. KMS Implementation Framework- Smuts, Hanlie & Van der Merwe, Alta & Loock, Marianne & Kotzé, Paula. (2009). A framework and methodology for knowledge management system implementation. ACM International Conference Proceeding Series. 70-79. 10.1145/1632149.1632160.

54. Knowledge Asset Management- Apostolou, Dimitris & Abecker, Andreas & Young, Ron. (2003). Knowledge Asset Management. 10.1007/978-1-4471-0069-0.

55. Onboarding and Learning Management- Karambelkar, M. and Bhattacharya, S. (2017), "Onboarding is a change: Applying change management model ADKAR to onboarding", Human Resource Management International Digest, Vol. 25 No. 7, pp. 5-8. https://doi.org/10.1108/HRMID-04-2017-0073

56. Learned Knowledge System- Lessons Learned Process. Originally published on January 4, 2017 | by Stan Garfield | Medium | https://stangarfield.medium.com/lessons-learned-process-dbc5743fb99b

57. Experts and Collaboration Systems- Wenger, Etienne & McDermott, Richard & Snyder, William. (2002). Cultivating Communities of Practice: A Guide to Managing Knowledge.

58. Knowledge Exchange Facilitation- Facilitator Guidelines (stanford.edu) | https://web.stanford.edu/group/resed/resed/staffresources/RM/training/facilguide.html

59. Competitive intelligence- Wikipedia

60. How To Facilitate A Successful Brainstorming Session | Articles | Chief Innovation Officer | Innovation Enterprise (theinnovationenterprise.com) | https://channels.

theinnovationenterprise.com/articles/how-to-facilitate-a-successful-brainstorming-session

61. Knowledge Spread- Nonaka, Ikujiro; Takeuchi, Hirotaka *(1995)*, The knowledge creating company: how Japanese companies create the dynamics of innovation, *New York: Oxford University Press, p. 284*, ISBN 978-0-19-509269-1

62. Taxonomy- Lambe, Patrick. (2007). Organizing Knowledge: Taxonomies, Knowledge and Organizational Effectiveness.

63. Key Critical Knowledge- Managing Your Mission-Critical Knowledge (hbr.org) 2015, martin Ihrig and Ian Macmilan

64. Just-in-Time Knowledge Visibility- Just-in-time manufacturing - Wikipedia | https://en.wikipedia.org/wiki/Just-in-time_manufacturing

65. Digital Knowledge Management- How Digital Knowledge Management is Foundational For Your Brand | Yext | https://www.yext.com/blog/2018/05/how-digital-knowledge-management-is-foundational-for-your-brand/

66. Building a Learning Organization- https://hbr.org/1993/07/building-a-learning-organization

67. Develop a KM Stragegy- Components of a KM Strategic Plan - knowledgemanagementdepot.com | https://knowledgemanagementdepot.com/2012/12/31/components-of-a-km-strategic-plan/

68. Physical/Virtual Knowledge *Cafés*- Gurteen Knowledge Café - Knowledge Café | http://knowledge.cafe/

69. Gemba Walks- Gemba - Wikipedia | https://en.wikipedia.org/wiki/Gemba#:

70. Knowledge Sharing Sessions- Knowledge sharing - Wikipedia | https://en.wikipedia.org/wiki/Knowledge_sharing

71. Classical and IT-based methods of KM practices- IS-43_KM-Tools_and_Techniques_2010.pdf (apo-tokyo. org) | https://www.apo-tokyo.org/00e-books/IS-43_KM-Tools_and_Techniques_2010/IS-43-KM-Tools_and_ Techniques_2010.pdf

72. Rewards and Recognition- Employee recognition - Wikipedia | https://en.wikipedia.org/wiki/Employee_recognition

73. KPI on the Metrics- Performance indicator - Wikipedia | https://en.wikipedia.org/wiki/Performance_indicator

74. 4 Core Processess- ISO - ISO 30401:2018 - Knowledge management systems — Requirements | https://www.iso. org/standard/68683.html

75. Knowledge Transfer Session - Knowledge transfer - Wikipedia

76. Transformational Tools- *Jakubik, Maria. (2007). Exploring the Knowledge Landscape: Four Emerging Views of Knowledge. Journal of Knowledge Management. 11. 10.1108/13673270710762675*

77. Adopted from ADB's Knowledge Solution (Image)- Source: http://ead.laboro.edu.br/knowledge-base-documents-search-hilti-india.pdf

78. Aspect of Knowledge Management- Anthony J. Reilly; v16. pdf (snu.edu) | https://home.snu.edu/~jsmith/library/ body/v16.pdf

79. Other Dimmensions- Shannak, Rifat. (2009). Measuring Knowledge Management Performance. European Journal of Scientific Research. 35. 242-253.

80. Knowledge Infrastructure- documents1.worldbank.org/ curated/en/757011518451751930/pdf/123393-WP-PUBLIC-AoKEGSURRGuideWeb.pdf

81. Artifical Intelligence Bases Systems- Aligning your KM and AI Strategies - knowledgemanagementdepot.com | http://knowledgemanagementdepot.com/2020/11/29/aligning-your-km-and-ai-strategies/

82. Augmented Reality- Augmented reality - Wikipedia

83. 5S- 5S (methodology) - Wikipedia | https://en.wikipedia.org/wiki/5S_(methodology)

84. Digital KM Solutions-

    1. Digital knowledge management – the key to business survival and success | Bdaily

    2. How Digital Knowledge Management is Foundational For Your Brand | Yext

    3. Interview with Jeffrey Rohrs, CMO at Yext | MarTech Advisor

85. Augmentation- Augmented reality - Wikipedia

86. Knowledge Visualization-

    1. Bertschi, Stefan & Bresciani, Sabrina & Crawford, Tom & Goebel, Randy & Kienreich, Wolfgang & Lindner, Martin & Sabol, Vedran & Vande Moere, Andrew. (2011). What is Knowledge Visualization? Perspectives on an Emerging Discipline. Proceedings of the International Conference on Information Visualisation. 329 - 336. 10.1109/IV.2011.5[8].

    2. Juan Gómez-Romero, Miguel Molina-Solana, Axel Oehmichen, Yike Guo,Visualizing large knowledge graphs: A performance analysis, Future Generation Computer Systems,Volume 8[9], 20[1]8, Pages 224-238, ISSN 0167-739X, https://doi.org/10.1016/j.future.2018.06.015.

87. Knowledge Societies- Understanding Knowledge Societies, United Nations ; https://publicadministration. un.org/publications/content/PDFs/E-Library%20 Archives/2005%20Understanding%20Knowledge%20 Societies.pdf

88. KM in Large Organizations- Program management and project portfolio management (pmi.org) | https://www.pmi. org/learning/library/new-competences-project-oriented-organizations-8938

89. Full-Time Employees- Berio, Giuseppe. (2006). Knowledge Management for Competence Management

90. Human Body Function- List of systems of the human body - Wikipedia

91. Intelligent Social Systems- Martela, Mikko & Saarinen, Esa. (2008). The Nature of Social Systems in Systems Intelligence: Insights from Intersubjective Systems Theory.

92. Knowledge Management- What is Knowledge Management? - Glossary - TOPdesk | https://www.topdesk.com/en/ glossary/what-is-knowledge-management/

93. At the National Level- KM- UAE | https://www.mof.gov.ae/ en/About/Development/Pages/KnowledgeManagement. aspx

94. Different Continents- KM IN Asia | https://www.apo-tokyo. org/publications/ebooks/knowledge-management-in-asia-experience-and-lessons-pdf-6-3mb/

95. Different Continents- European Union KM policy | https:// publications.jrc.ec.europa.eu/repository/bitstream/ JRC110151/2017-12-07_a3-leaflet_km-infographics.pdf

96. Knowledge Management at Every Level of Human Existence- The Art of Knowledge Exchange: A Results-Focused Planning Guide for Development Practitioners, Second

Edition Updated | https://openknowledge.worldbank.org/handle/10986/17540

97. Knowledge Management at Every Level of Human Existence-KNOWLEDGE MANAGEMENT IN THE UNITED NATIONS SYSTEM | https://www.unjiu.org/sites/www.unjiu.org/files/jiu_document_files/products/en/reports-notes/JIU%20Products/JIU_REP_2016_10_English.pdf

98. KM Strategy for Agriculture Development | https://webapps.ifad.org/members/eb/126/docs/EB-2019-126-R-2-Rev-1.pdf

99. Food and agriculture organization - UN – FAO | http://www.fao.org/fileadmin/user_upload/knowledge/docs/ABC_of_KM.pdf

100. Microsoft SharePoint- What is SharePoint? - Office Support (microsoft.com)

101. Contextual and Organization Development- Breakthrough in Organization Development by R. R. Blake, J. S. Mouton,L. B. Barnes, and L. E. Greiner | https://hbr.org/1964/11/breakthrough-in-organization-development

102. Communication- Knoco stories: 6 principles of KM communication (nickmilton.com) | http://www.nickmilton.com/2019/09/6-principles-of-km-communication.html

103. Documentation- Jay Schlickman, (2003); ISO 9001:2000 -Quality Management System Design

104. Sarbanes–Oxley Act - Wikipedia | https://en.wikipedia.org/wiki/Sarbanes%E2%80%93Oxley_Act

105. Records management - Wikipedia | https://en.wikipedia.org/wiki/Records_management

106. Customer-Centric KM- Hadi, Nejatian & Khalilabad, & Mazandarani, Omid & Ilham, Sentosa & Piaralal, Shishi.

(2006). The Impact of Knowledge Management on Customer Relationship Management

107. Product-Based KM- Ng, Poh Kiat & Goh, Gerald & Eze, Uchenna. (2011). The Role Of Knowledge Management In Product Development Performance: A Review. Journal of Knowledge Management Practice. 12

108. Measurement of Engagement- Fletcher, Luke & Robinson, Dilys. (2014). Measuring and Understanding Engagement. 10.4324/9780203076965

109. CoPs- Smits, Martin & Moor, Aldo. (2004). Measuring Knowledge Management Effectiveness in Communities of Practice. 10.1109/HICSS.2004.1265570.

110. Measurement of Collaboration- Stephen Michael Impink, Andrea Prat, and Raffaella Sadun (2020); Measuring Collaboration in Modern Organizations (hbs.edu) | https://www.hbs.edu/faculty/Publication%20Files/ MeasuringCollaboration_May2020_e5654df5-2f2e-4752-aa23-67c05e167107.pdf

111. Measurement of Knowledge Innovation- Leber, Marjan & Buchmeister, Borut & Ivanisevic, Andrea. (2015). Impact of Knowledge on Innovation Process. 10.2507/daaam. scibook.2015.21.

APPENDIX I

10 STEPS GUIDE TO DESIGN KM SYSTEM

	10 Steps- Guide to roll out KM System	Yes/No	Remarks
1	Develop Business Case for the Function/Knowledge Entity		
2	Capture the Knowledge Landscape of the function/Knowledge Entity		
3	Develop use case of Circle of Knowledge based on KE		
4	Mapping taxonomy/Taskonomy involving – Assets, Artifacts Type, Experts, Geographical locations, working units, etc.		
5	Proposing KM solutions, Choosing 1 or 2 areas to prototype		
6	Engage with multiple stakeholders during the design phase, communication and change management		

	10 Steps- Guide to roll out KM System	*Yes/ No*	*Remarks*
7	Develop KM solutions – systems, processes, practices, procedures, KPIs, governance, etc.		
8	Operationalize KM systems, manage content and relevancy, user rights, value creation out of the system		
9	Review the value out of these initiatives, report to management		
10	Continuous Improvement of the KM system based on User requirements		

KEY CONCEPTS IN KM LIFECYCLE

Initiate	<ul><li>Knowledge management stand-alone</li><li>KM function-driven/ group-driven</li><li>Knowledge management services</li><li>Knowledge management services at the enterprise level</li><li>Knowledge management consulting</li><li>Knowledge management workshops</li><li>Knowledge management facilitation</li><li>Knowledge management systems that service collaborative spaces, knowledge services</li><li>Taxonomy development services</li><li>KM repository that requires document management is a system</li><li>KM product development, new R&D areas</li><li>KM practices development</li><li>KM framework developments, technology and services</li></ul>	

Plan	<ul><li>KM strategy</li><li>KM operational excellence</li><li>KM systems architecture and Knowledge Experience</li><li>KM processes</li><li>KM content</li><li>KM interfaces</li><li>KM projects and program</li><li>KM governance</li><li>KM culture and change management</li><li>Organizational development and emerging technologies</li><li>Strategic level planning,</li><li>Tactical level planning,</li><li>Operational level planning,</li><li>Governance level planning.</li><li>People engagement and change management planning,</li><li>Communication planning,</li><li>KM technology planning, and</li><li>KM practices planning.</li></ul>	
Design	<ul><li>Enterprise KM</li><li>Management Steering Committee</li><li>KM Function</li><li>KM initiatives</li><li>Enterprise-wide</li><li>Business/Service Unit-wide</li><li>Group/Team/Department-wide</li><li>KM Programs</li><li>Staggered KM Programs</li></ul>	

		• Continuous KM Program
		• KM Projects
		• Long-Term KM Projects
		• Short-Term KM Projects
		• Medium-Term KM Projects
		• KM systems
		• Ad-Hoc
		• Stand-alone
		• KM initiatives
		• Knowledge management
		• KM Driven Nationally
		• KM category
		• General KM
		• Classic KM
		• Advanced KM
Design		• Futuristic KM
		• KM Functional Process
		• Processes on developing KM Framework at the highest level
		• Processes on KM system lifecycle management
		• Processes on KM development process-creation, development, reuse, archival supporting activities with respect to KM systems
		• KM Processes being embedded in the business process as a checklist or mandatory requirements depending on the severity of the knowledge process
		• Processes to measure, evaluate and improve the KM systems

Implement			
	Operation	Support Group/Project/Individual Level KM KMS standalone Enterprise KM National KM KM Competency Development Technical Path in Knowledge Management Facilitation Knowledge Management Path Content - Knowledge Management Path KM Support Path Program Management Path or Leadership Knowledge Management Path Research and Innovation KM Path Change Management/Communication Path Awareness and Communication	
	Continuous Improvement	Performance Evaluation • Measurement of Engagement – what is the kind of engagement a KM Program/ system is able to generate • Measurement of Effectiveness- How effective is the KMS to the user, or what value is the KM creating for the user • Measurement of Collaboration- How are people collaborating among each other, what results are they producing it	

Continuous Improvement	• Measurement of Knowledge Experience- How does one experience the ease of knowledge access and visibility around them and also have access to it • Measurement of Knowledge Innovation – How Organization are managing knowledge to create an innovation culture	

APPENDIX III

KMS IMPLEMENTATION CHECKLIST

Cl- Clauses Number, sub-clause; App/NA – Applicable or Not Applicable

2	Plan Phase Procedures steps:	Cl	App /NA	Comments
	• Develop Organization/ Functional Decomposition Mapping			
	• Identify Key Stakeholders/ Interested Parties			
	• Develop Knowledge Proximity Order matrix – for interested parties engaging them in workshops			
	• Develop detailed 8 Folds KM Planning			
	• Develop a RACI Matrix for the organization			

Phase Input:			
• Organization's Decomposition Mapping Documents			
• Functional Decomposition Mapping Documents			
• Knowledge Proximity Order Matrix Document			
• Minutes			
• Survey Forms			
• Interview Transcript			
Phase Outputs:			
• Business Case for KM program/ Initiative			
• Business KM Requirements Documents			
• KM Architecture Planning Document			
• KM Blueprint Documents			
• Team Workspaces			
• Document Sharing Workspace			
• Forums to discuss them			
Guides/SOP			
• Organization Decomposition Procedures			
• Functional Decomposition Procedure			
• KM Self-Assessment Report			
• KM Road Map Document			
• KM Proximity Order Matrix Procedure			

Template			
• Organization Decomposition Template			
• Functional Decomposition template			
• Action Tracker Template			
• KM Architecture Planning template			
• RACI Matrix Templates			
• Minutes of Meetings Template			
• Establish the Role of KM SPOCS for KM Systems/Initiatives in every function or knowledge entities			
Foundation Block 1: **Establish Knowledge Asset Management program**			
• Conduct Knowledge Asset Management (KAM)			
• Workshop/Engagement Sessions			
• The KAM workshop may span over multiple working sessions			
• KAM could be at the Macro or Micro–level			
• In the Workshops/Engagement Sessions			
• Determine the Approach needed			
• Determine the Organizational Area			
• Determine the KAM Solution			
• Design KAM Solution			
• Design KAM System			

• Design KPI			
• Design Evangelization Plan			
• Plan for Operationalization and Support			
Foundation Block 2: **Establish Onboarding and Learning Management**			
• Determine Competency and Skills requirement			
• Design Onboarding Systems to reduce the learning curve			
• Establish Subject and Topic-Based Forums			
• Design Macro and Micro Onboarding System			
• Establish Internal and External Collaboration			
• Establish Local, Regional and International collaboration			
• Plan for Operationalization and Support			
Foundation Block 3: **Establish a Lesson Learned Knowledge system**			
• Conduct LL Workshop to gather requirements			
• Establish the Change Management Process			
• Design the LL System, LL Process and LL Deployment Plan			
• Develop KPI Systems			

• Facilitate Peer-to-Peer Sharing Workshops			
• Plan for Operationalization and Support			
Foundation block* 4: **Establish Experts and Collaboration Systems**			
• Map Expertise			
• Develop Expertise Map			
• Develop CoPs			
• Mature CoPs			
• Plan for Operationalization and Support			
• Guidelines			
Phase Inputs			
• Templates filled by interested parties			
• Conversations feedback			
• Forums feedback			
• Surveys outcomes			
• Meetings outcomes			
Phase Outputs			
• Foundational KM System Solution Design			
• Developing Knowledge Asset Management System Procedures			
• Developing Onboarding and Learning Management System Procedures			
• Lesson Learned Knowledge System Implementation Procedure			

• Developing Expert Systems and CoP's Implementation Procedures			
• Moderators and Users Guides			
• Knowledge Exchange Facilitation			
• Lesson Workshop Facilitation Guidelines			
• Innovation and Knowledge Strategy Facilitation Guidelines			
• Highly Effective Knowledge Sharing Workshops			
• Enhanced Collaboration with Interested Parties			
• Taxonomy Mapping			
• Knowledge Asset Mapping			
• Process Asset Mapping			
• Work-Activities-Tasks Mapping			
• Process Documentation Mapping			
• Technical Documentation			
• Skills and Development Roadmap			
• Resources and Mentor Mapping			
• Lesson Capture Process Development			
• Lessons Reuse Process Declaration			
• Organizational Learning Embedding Tracker			
• Experts Profiling Template			

• Themes Setup Questionnaire			
• Peer-to-Peer Sharing Templates			
• Lessons Review Templates			
• Innovation and Knowledge Management Development Working Sheets			
• Taxonomy Development Working Sheet			
1. Implement,			
2. Operation and			
3. Continuous Improvement			

The first thing you have to start after the initial kick-off meetings, to analyze:

1. What is the existing knowledge infrastructure?		
2. What are the processes that are defined to capture, share, store knowledge?		
3. What are the key processes leading to knowledge?		
4. How do you document the changes?		
5. Who are the experts in this field of marketing/sales team?		
6. Where do the team members find their documents?		
7. Where do the team members find artifacts?		
8. Where do they find the external links and the customer contacts, ct cetera?		

9. Where do the product teams communicate?		
10. How do they communicate?		
11. What are the various internal, external communications and where are they stored?		
12. In what format are they stored, etc.?		
13. How do you find competitive intelligence (CI)about the competitors?		
14. What mechanism or process or system is available to provide the CI?		
15. How do you train the new member or how do you onboard a new member?		
16. What are the methods and practices at present?		
17. How do you manage and learn from customer interactions?		
18. What are the various digital spaces?		
19. What are the physical spaces?		
20. Which are the portals the team uses?		
21. Where do they and how do they collect the materials for the onboarding?		
22. What is the training for the people, to people, is digital training in place?		

23. Are the lessons captured currently?		
24. How is the sharing happening within the team, etc.?		
The Policy		
• What is your KM vision?		
• What is your policy on KM performance management?		
• What is your KM storage policy?		
• What is your KM review on the archival policy?		
• What is your knowledge creation policy?		
• What is your knowledge management policy?		
• What are your controls and knowledge as a part of the policy?		
• What is your KM backup policy?		
• What is the KM access control policy?		
• What is your policy on KM communications?		
• What are your storage and guidelines policy?		
• What are your change management guidelines?		
• What are your good practices and learning islands?		
• What are your technology and definitions for the KM (Glossaries)?		

• What are the KM access control procedures?		
• What are your communication procedures?		
• What is your KM orientation program?		
• How do you change management?		
• What is your change management procedure?		
• What are knowledge management, knowledge creation procedures?		
• What are the KM review procedures?		
• What are the story procedures and what are the backup policies?		
• Roles, Responsibility and Authorities		
• When to report, what is the frequency of reporting?		
• How is the performance measured?		
• What criteria are defined as KM measurement, etc.,		
• How do we overcome this challenge?		
• What methods are required?		
• How to drive KM effectiveness at the end of the day?		

	• How do you make KM relevant to leadership, middle management and managers?		

Create the Required Foundational Block based on the industry and organization challenges;

Planning			
	• What is the KM strategy for the organization?		
	• What are various KM entities?		
	• What should be the strategy to assess requirements?		
	• What should be the tactical way of handling it?		
	• How do you develop KM technology solutions?		
	• How do you have the right people doing the KM function?		
	• What kind of skills, competencies, experiences are needed to fit the development of the KM ecosystem?		
	• What kind of environment does the management need to develop to establish KM culture?		
	• What kind of investment is required to establish a full-fledged KM function and associated technologies?		
	• How many FTEs are needed to drive KM in this form at the strategic level?		
	• What are the business challenges in hand?		

• What are the available KM solutions?		
• Do IT-KM systems need customization?		
• Does it meet the needed out-of-the-box configuration?		
• How do we develop taxonomy for the business unit to manage critical knowledge assets, process assets, expertise mapping, and build communities and conversations to mentor and guide?		
• How to plan the implementation of KMs?		
• What are the challenges or pitfalls of implementing this program to all the knowledge management tools?		
• What strategy should be devised to overcome these pitfalls?		
• How to energize the project leadership, product team managers in this process of development, then what are their needs at that level?		
• And what are the challenges in terms of the knowledge domain?		
• How do you plan their mutual collaboration mechanism?		
• What are the challenges, how to overcome these challenges?		
• What are the catalysts who are the catalysts who could provide the guidance and lead in a business bind?		

• What are the key demands?		
• How can they build the support teams, supporting the initiative?		
• How can they develop people who want to contribute to this initiative?		
• What are the needs? How do you capture the needs?		
• How to create the KM solutions catalog?		
• How to develop the technology of KM-based practices or KM practices, non-tech people, tech-people?		
• How to develop procedures and manuals for the users when it comes to project or the grass-root level, there need to be other plans in place, exams, communication plan, change management plan, people engagement plan, etc.?		
• Why launch KM?		
• How do you launch the KM system?		
• Who are your primary audiences?		
• What communication do you plan to send?		
• What is that, I mean, what design elements are you going to use?		
• How are you going to develop manuals and documentation for usage? What are the other KM practices being defined?		

• How to nominate experts for knowledge sharing?		
• How many usable artifacts should have been controverted?		
• How many knowledge assets should I have contributed?		
• Learn how many mentees need to be trained. How to groom and train the rookies?		
• Who are the experts? That in point, what level of expert competency and skills they need to be trained in?		
• What are the key lessons being shared, and when do they need to share?		
• How are the teams supposed to communicate updates within the team, external to the team and vice versa?		
• How can leaders manage solid leads that everybody knows within the team?		
• How do you encourage the team to call the higher management to celebrate success?		
• What are the Rewards and Recognition devised?		
• What are the Reward and Recognition given for the highest KM value generators, and how do you provide encouragement to knowledge consumers?		
• How many publications or what newsletters or content cards are the teams supposed to be provided, etc.?		

	• How to develop KPIs on the metrics?		
	• How to capture the effectiveness of KM system practices in the KM function?		
	• How to capture the data point, pints of the number of case studies, best practices, IPs, patents, frameworks, guides, updates, communication, newsletter, knowledge assets, Communities of Practice, LL workshops, peer-to-peer workshops?		
	• How do you capture the voice of customers and make it to the dashboard?		
	• How do you get feedback on KM practices and develop it?		
Knowledge Conveyance and Transformation			
	• What are the various KM Tools and Methods? Why to use these methods and tools?		
	• Does it need deep Cultural Change Management?		
	• What are the interventions needed to bring teams together and do community learning?		
	• Does the team spend too much time searching for valid content and is it difficult for the team to find the content?		
	• Is the team finding the communications thwarted when it comes to new products, updates, etc.?		

• Are the learning and sharing not happening between two projects, two functions, between multiple team members?		
• Is the tacit experience of teams not captured effectively for organizational dissemination?		
• Is the feedback from the market and customers not able to develop competitive intelligence?		

Support		
• Does the organization have a budget for KM function, system and team?		
• Will the management drive KM culture and steer the program?		
• Does the person chosen to facilitate knowledge management design understands the industry-standard technology, business, people, and has management support?		
• Do you have the tools, methodology, framework, approaches, and way of doing things to facilitate the knowledge sharing, knowledge creation, knowledge reuse, harvesting, and knowledge archiving processes, methods in place?		
• Do you have people who would create, develop the KM practices as a way of life in this transactional corporate world?		

• Do you have people driving KM in Initiative?		
• What support do they need?		
• What resources do they need?		
• Teach them KM principal and create an eco-system to develop knowledge management solutions with classical methods and technology-oriented practices.		
• Does the person who is going to lead KM has previous experience in the KM domain or has the ability to lead?		
• Does he have the flare to understand the business context and deliver results appropriately?		
• What are the success rates in past? What documentation can prove his capabilities and experience? Does he have experience in managing programs, teams, technologies, KM solutions?		
Enterprise KM		
• What are the KM digital systems?		
• How are the KM functions aligned with marketing, communication context in which the KM analyst is needed?		
• What if your organization does not have a formal KM?		
• It is important to think about what if you are enveloped in challenges in the context of receiving critical documents?		

Role-based KM		
• How do I perform this task?		
• How do I perform this activity?		
• How do I ask, "Where are these application links?" "I am not able to find the digital format."		
• How to ask my manager?		
• How do I ask this question to any of my colleagues?		
• How to find relevant experiential knowledge in this work area management?		
Internal Audit		
• What to look at from the KM scope?		
• How KMS is impacting?		
• How are the solutions making a difference in the organization?		
• How's the management supporting the KM initiative?		
• What are the effects of knowledge sharing in the organization?		
• How is the conversation flowing in the organization, is it engaging, encouraging making mistake, or it is a punishing culture?		
• What are the multiple aspects of KM principles playing in the background?		

APPENDIX IV

LIST OF KM METHODS AND TOOLS*

C- Creation | M- Manage | A-Apply | Retain-R | Purge/ Archive -P

KM Tools and Methods	C	M	A	R	P
After Action Reviews					
Blogs					
Body of Knowledge					
Brainstorming					
Building Knowledge Clusters					
Collaboration Spaces					
Collaborative Physical Workspaces					
Collaborative Virtual Workspaces					
Communities of Practice					
Conferences					
Content Management System					
Document Libraries					
Expertise Locator/Who's Who					
Good Practices /Best Practices					

Knowledge Assessment Tool					
Knowledge asset management systems					
Knowledge Augmented Reality					
Knowledge Bases (Wikis, etc.)					
Knowledge Café					
Knowledge Chatbots					
Knowledge Clusters					
Knowledge Database					
Knowledge Discovery Workshops					
Knowledge Fair					
Knowledge Gamification					
Knowledge Graph					
Knowledge Jam					
Knowledge Mapping					
Knowledge Portal					
Knowledge Portal Video Sharing Mentor/ Mentee Scheme					
Knowledge Quiz					
Knowledge Repositories					
Knowledge seminars					
Knowledge Sharing Sessions					
Knowledge Visualization					
Knowledge Webcast/Podcast					
Knowledge Worker Competency Plan					
Learning Reviews					
Learning Reviews After Action Reviews					
Learnings and Ideas Capture					
Lesson Learned Workshops					
Maturity Model					
Mentor/Mentee Scheme					

Mind Map					
Peer Assist					
Peer Sharing					
Record Management System					
Reusable Knowledge Assets					
Social Network Services					
Storytelling					
Taxonomy Development Workshop					
Unconference					
Video Communication and Webinars					
Video Sharing					
Advanced Search Tools					
AI-Based Search					
Case Studies					
Center of Excellence					
Communities of Interest					
Competency Management					
Knowledge Retention					
Lunch and Learn					
Mentor/Mentee Scheme Knowledge Portal					
Wiki					
Taskonomy					
Knowledge Purging/Archiving					

*- Few Examples

TAXONOMY DEVELOPMENT EXAMPLE FOR CREATING HIGHLY VISIBLE CONTENTS WITHIN SMALL GROUPS AND LARGE GROUPS- FUNDAMENTAL BLOCK OF KM

Marketing/ Sales	Market Intelligence	Marketing Collateral Management	Account Intelligence
	Media & PR Management	Clippings	Account snapshot
	Analyst Management	Print References	Account dossiers
	Advisory Management	Brochures	Outside-in analysis
	Account Real Estate Management		
	Accounting & Expenses Management		
	Event & Roadshow Management		
	Deal Intelligence	**Geo/Location Intelligence**	**Competitive Intelligence**
	Battle Cards	BPO-IT Market Trends	Competitive Finance
	Win/Loss Reports	Service Lines Reports	Competitors
		Geo Reports	Global Competitors
		Industry Reports	Indian Competitors
			Regional Vendors

	Analyst Management	Advisory Management	Sales Management
	Collaterals	Reports	Account Real Estate
	Who's Who	Collaterals	Sales Dashboard & MIS
	Assets	Who's Who	Order Book Forecasting
	Presentations	Assets	Sales Activity Update
		Presentations	New Account Addition
	Demand Management	**Account Management**	**Opportunity Management**
	Prospecting	Account Planning	Opportunity Generation
	How do I run Campaign Event	Master Service Agreement	Order Entry & Amendments
		Relationship Management	Proposal Response
		Account intelligence	Bid Assessments
		Account Profitability Calculators	Statement of Work
			Opportunity Qualification
			Contract Negotiation
			Deal Risk Evaluation
			Win-Loss Reviews

THANK YOU

Thank You for Reading My Book!

I really appreciate all of your feedback,
and would love to hear what you have to say.

I welcome your input to make the next edition of this book
and my future books even better.

Please leave me a helpful review on Amazon,
letting me know what you think of the book.

Thank you so much!
Santhosh Shekar